CW01262950

What on Earth!

What are you interested in? This might be the most important question you ever ask yourself. All our books at What on Earth! are designed to help you explore and discover whatever fascinates you most. And when you share your discoveries with others, your joy spreads far and wide. Because, when it comes right down to it...
the real world is far more amazing than anything you can make up!

Christopher Lloyd
Founder, What on Earth!

For my amazing granddaughter
Lorenza Inez Tomecek, who has all the right
stuff to make our world a better place!
– Steve

For Conor and Alyson
– John

THE GREATEST STUFF ON EARTH

THE AMAZING SCIENCE OF SUNLIGHT, SMARTPHONES, MICROPHONES, MUSHROOMS & EVERYTHING IN BETWEEN

WRITTEN BY STEVE TOMECEK
ILLUSTRATED BY JOHN DEVOLLE

What on Earth!

We often think of stuff as the objects we buy and use, like this skateboarder's board, clothes, and watch. But stuff is so much more. The pavement he's skating on and the buildings around him are all made of stuff. The ground, the air, and the sunlight are, too. His body is stuff, as are the Earth, the solar system and the whole vast universe!

INTRODUCTION

We live in a world surrounded by lots of different stuff. Some, like the air we breathe and the water we drink, is found in nature, and we need it for our very survival. Other stuff, like the paper in this book or the clothing you wear or the smartphones people are constantly staring at, were invented by people and help to make our lives more comfortable and enjoyable.

This book tells the story of all the incredible stuff that we humans use and depend on as we go about our daily lives. Along the way, you'll discover how stuff originally formed and how people learned to change some natural stuff into new stuff altogether.

Because there are so many different types of stuff, it would be impossible to cover everything in one book. Instead, I'll highlight some of the stuff that has had big impacts on humans and the way we live. I will also look at some of the problems that having too much of the wrong stuff has caused and how creative people are working to solve those problems.

Welcome to The Greatest Stuff on Earth!

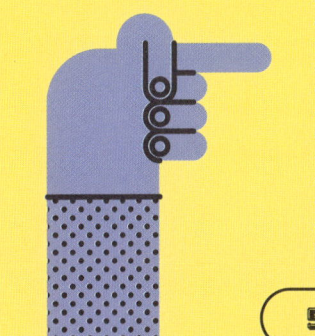

CONTENTS

5 INTRODUCTION

8 STUFF: THE BASICS

10 SOMETIMES IT'S MATTER
12   Atoms & Elements
14   Compounds
16 OTHER TIMES IT'S ENERGY

20 NATURE STUFF

22 IT CAME FROM THE BIG BANG
24   Stars
26 THE GROUND BENEATH US – ROCKS
28   Magnets
30 YUM... DIRT
32 AWASH IN WATER
34   Frozen
35   Recycled
36 LIFE-GIVING LIGHT
38 WEATHER-FILLED AIR
40   Our Greenhouse
42   Fire
44 THE COOLEST FEAT – LIFE
46   DNA
48   Cells
50   Chloroplasts
52   Mitochondria
54   Microbes

56 STUFF HUMANS MAKE & USE

58 FABULOUS FOOD
60 Nutrients
62 Food & Fire
64 Ovens
65 Pots & Pans
66 Preserving Food
68 Refrigeration

70 FEELING FUELISH
72 Alternative Energy
74 Electricity
76 Batteries

78 GIVE ME SHELTER
80 Building Materials

82 COVER UP WITH CLOTHES
84 First Fabrics

86 SPIN THE WHEEL
88 Motors

90 THE WRITE STUFF – PAPER
92 Type
93 The Printing Press

94 HERE'S TO YOUR HEALTH!
96 Disinfectants
98 Germ Fighters
100 Painkillers
102 Replacement Body Parts

104 LIGHTS, CAMERA, SMARTPHONE!
106 Mics & Speakers
108 Connections

110 PROBLEMS WITH STUFF

114 But There's More Stuff!
116 Glossary
120 Note on the Research
121 Selected Sources
123 Photo Credits
124 Index

STUF

F: THE BASICS

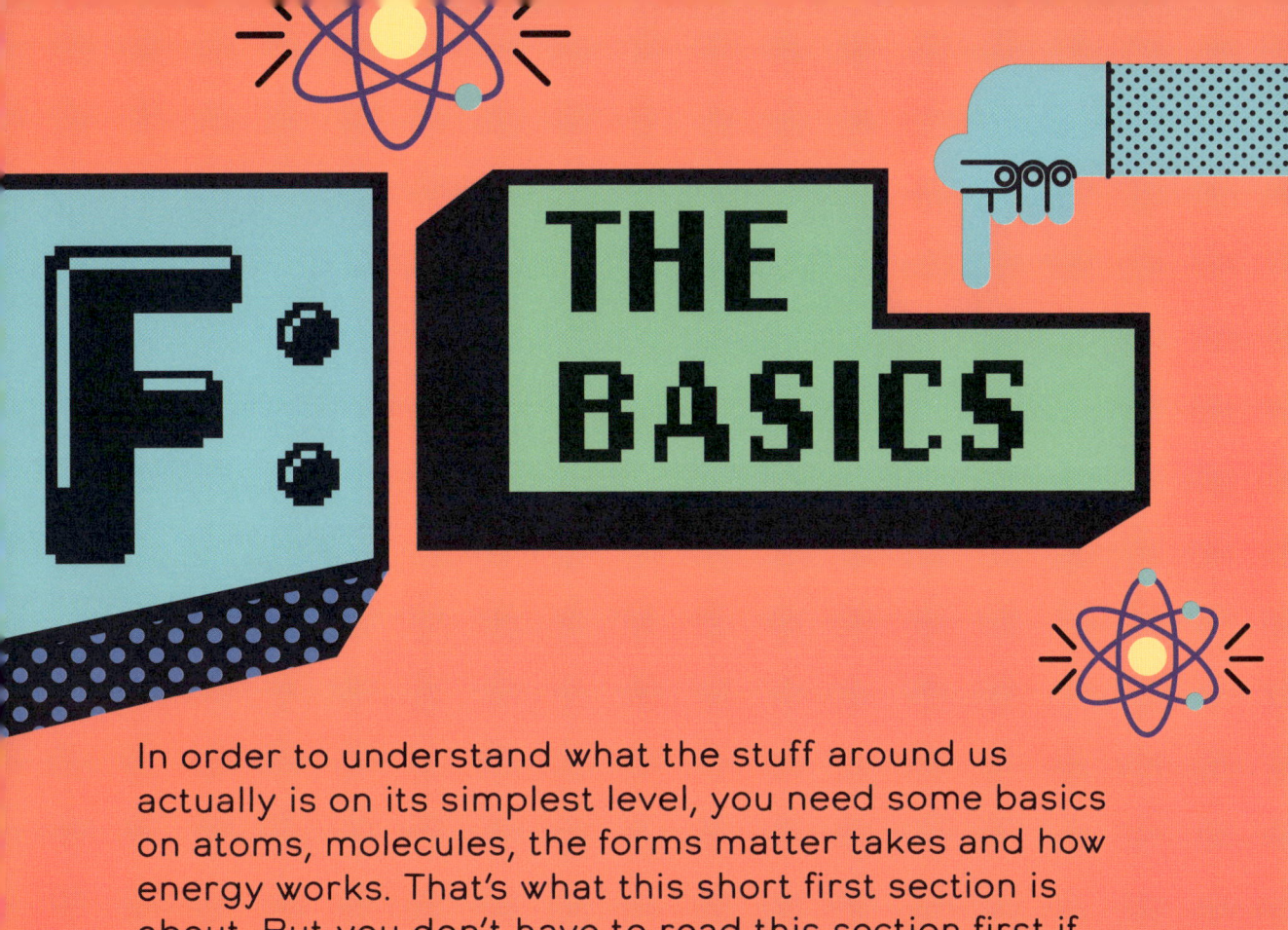

In order to understand what the stuff around us actually is on its simplest level, you need some basics on atoms, molecules, the forms matter takes and how energy works. That's what this short first section is about. But you don't have to read this section first if you don't feel like it. You can skip around the book, read other parts, and come back here when you need to. It's entirely up to you. I'll point you back to this section when I think it might be useful.

To get started, you need to know about two very important types of stuff: matter and energy. Matter is something made of atoms, so it has what we call 'mass'. It also takes up space. Energy is the stuff that makes matter move and change. Possibly the most amazing thing about matter and energy is that they can transform into one another. More on that later.

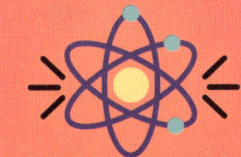

SOMETIMES IT'S MATTER

Matter is something made of atoms. Every bit of stuff in the form of matter has its own special set of properties, which describe how it looks or behaves. Properties can include size, shape, colour, texture and even smell. But in order for something to be matter, it must have two key properties. It must take up space and have mass. Mass is a measure of just how much stuff is found in something. Here on Earth, we calculate it by weighing that thing on a scale.

Matter also comes in different states. When we talk about a state of matter, we're describing the physical form that the matter takes. The four most common states of matter found here on Earth are solid, liquid, gas and plasma.

BONUS!

Our Sun is often described as a big ball of burning gas, but that's not correct! Our Sun, like all stars, is really a big ball of glowing plasma!

STUFF: THE BASICS

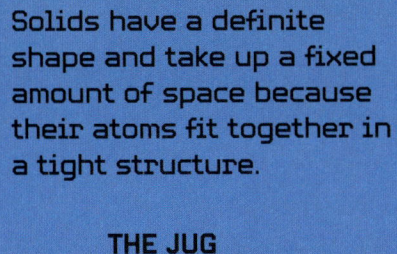

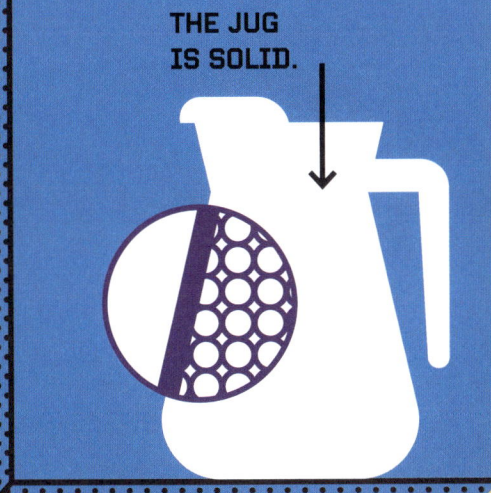

Solids have a definite shape and take up a fixed amount of space because their atoms fit together in a tight structure.

THE JUG IS SOLID.

Liquids take up a fixed amount of space, but flow to take the shape of the container.

THE WATER IS LIQUID.

Gases don't have either a fixed shape or a fixed volume. Their atoms spread out into the space around them.

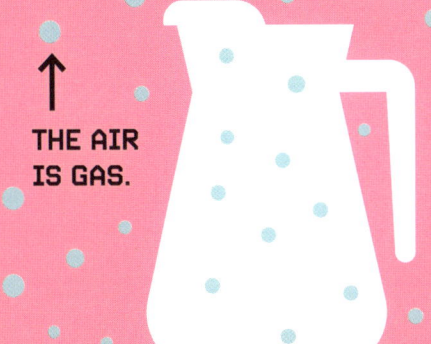

THE AIR IS GAS.

Lightning is plasma – a very hot gas-like substance that glows and is made of electrically charged particles (more about electrical charge on page 42).

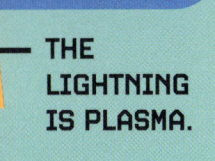

THE LIGHTNING IS PLASMA.

11

ATOMS & ELEMENTS

All matter is made of atoms, and different kinds of atoms (called chemical elements) make different kinds of matter.

Atoms vary in size, but they all are incredibly small. A typical atom is about 0.3 nanometres wide, which means that more than 40 million of them would fit across your thumb!

Most atoms have two main parts. At the centre of each atom is a nucleus, which usually has two types of particles – positively charged protons, and neutrons, which have no charge. Whizzing around the outside of the nucleus is a cloud of negatively charged electrons. Protons, neutrons and electrons are all known as subatomic particles.

The atom of each chemical element has its own atomic number based on the number of protons found in its nucleus. In a neutral atom, the number of protons equals the number of electrons orbiting the nucleus.

At least 92 chemical elements are found in nature (although scientists have discovered a few more in the lab).

The element helium has an atomic number of 2 because it has two protons in its nucleus, while the element carbon has an atomic number of 6 because it has six protons in its nucleus.

- — ELECTRON
- + — PROTON
- — NEUTRON
- — NUCLEUS

← HELIUM ATOM

CARBON ATOM →

STUFF: THE BASICS

13

COMPOUNDS

Few things exist as pure chemical elements made up of only one type of atom. Metals such as gold, copper and silver do. And so do gases such as hydrogen and helium. But most of the stuff that we encounter in our daily lives is made of chemical compounds. A compound is created when more than one type of atom joins together in a process called bonding.

Ionic Compounds

Some chemical compounds are called ionic compounds. Ions are chemical elements that have either gained or lost some of their electrons. When an atom loses electrons, it becomes positively charged. When an atom gains extra electrons, it becomes negatively charged. Positively charged ions and negatively charged ions are attracted to each other. They stick together, creating an ionic bond.

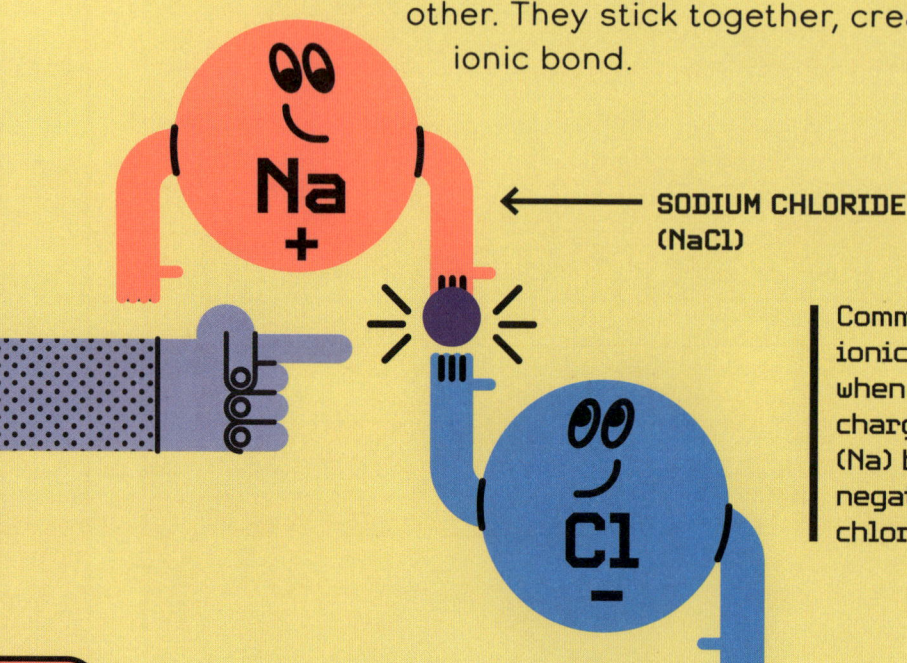

← SODIUM CHLORIDE (NaCl)

Common table salt is an ionic compound formed when a positively charged sodium ion (Na) bonds with a negatively charged chlorine ion (Cl).

Molecules

OXYGEN MOLECULE (O$_2$) →

Other atoms stick together by sharing electrons. This is called a molecular bond, and the combination of atoms is called a molecule. Some molecules are compounds and some aren't. Most of the oxygen we breathe is in the form of molecules. Each oxygen molecule is made of two oxygen atoms sharing electrons. Water is a molecule, too, but it is also a compound because it is a combination of more than one element. A single molecule of water is made of two hydrogen atoms bonded to a single oxygen atom.

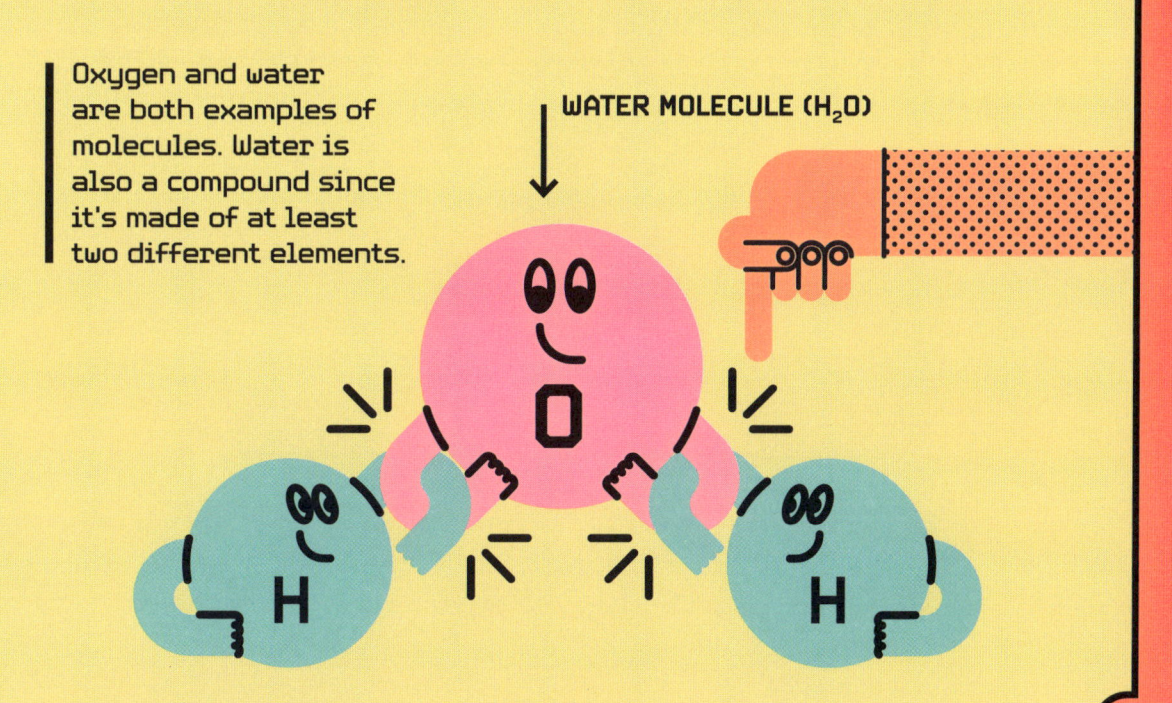

| Oxygen and water are both examples of molecules. Water is also a compound since it's made of at least two different elements.

WATER MOLECULE (H$_2$O) ↓

STUFF: THE BASICS

15

OTHER TIMES IT'S
ENERGY

The other main form stuff takes is energy. Energy makes things move and change. There are many types of energy, which move things, heat things, power living things or machines, and make things happen in other ways, too. The most important thing about energy is that it cannot be created or destroyed. Instead, it can change from one form of energy to another or into matter. Energy can also be transferred, or moved, from one object to another.

Here are six major types of energy:

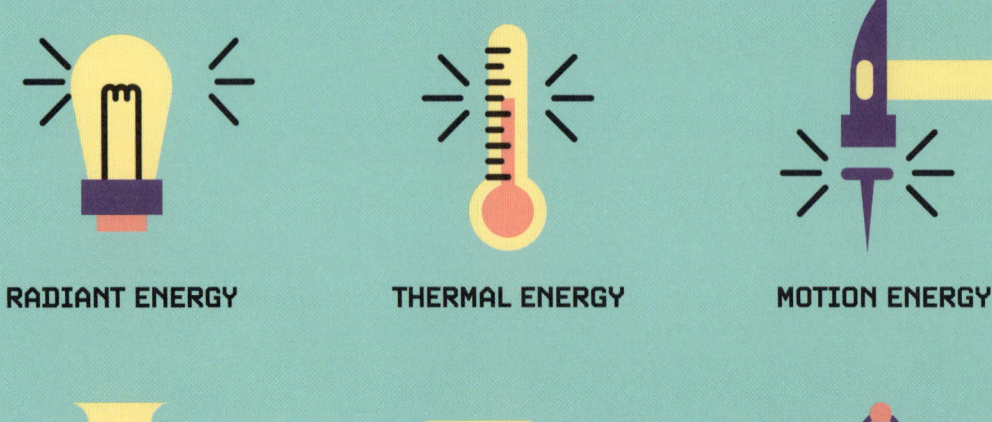

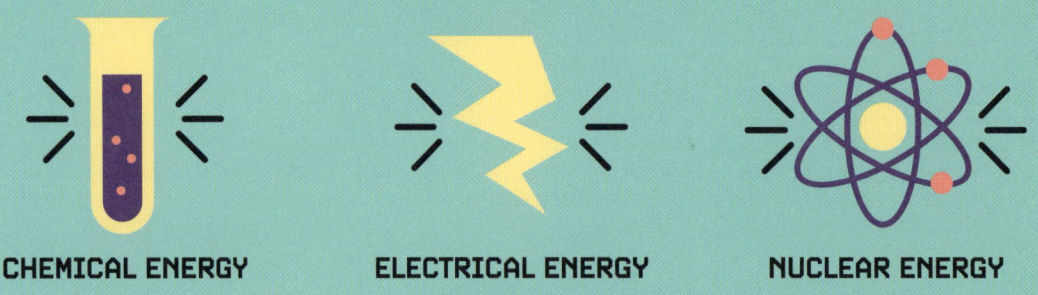

RADIANT ENERGY

THERMAL ENERGY

MOTION ENERGY

CHEMICAL ENERGY

ELECTRICAL ENERGY

NUCLEAR ENERGY

STUFF: THE BASICS

Radiant energy from the Sun provides plants with the energy they need to grow.

Radiant Energy

Radiant energy basically means light. Without radiant energy, most life on Earth would not exist. That's because sunlight is what powers photosynthesis, which allows plants and other life forms to grow.

Radiant energy also keeps our planet warm through a process called the greenhouse effect.

Go to page 50 for more about photosynthesis and to page 40 for more about the greenhouse effect.

Thermal Energy

Another name for thermal energy is 'heat'. We use it to keep warm, cook food, and manufacture all sorts of useful products. Thermal energy can come from lots of sources, including sunlight, electricity, and fire. Jump to page 62 to find out about cooking, one of the things we use thermal energy for.

Thermal energy is used for making many different products including steel, which you can see in its hot liquid form in this photo.

The wind supplies motion energy to turn these wind turbines. We'll have more on wind energy on page 72.

Motion Energy

Motion energy happens when something moves. When you throw a ball or hammer a nail, you are using motion energy. When you ride a skateboard down a hill, the motion energy is supplied by gravity.

Sound is a special type of motion energy. Sounds happen because an object is made to vibrate, or shake back and forth. The vibrations eventually reach our ears as pulses of energy in the air called sound waves.

Chemical Energy

Chemical energy is stored in the bonds that hold matter together. Breaking those bonds releases it and turns it into other forms of energy. Fire happens when the bonds in a fuel (such as wood) break and the chemical energy turns into radiant and thermal energy (light and heat).

Food contains chemical energy that powers our bodies. Batteries transform chemical energy into electrical energy.

Chemical energy is stored in fuels (such as this charcoal) until it is transformed into other forms of energy (such as thermal energy to cook your burger).

These days we are surrounded by devices powered by electrical energy.

Electrical Energy

Electricity comes from the movement of electrons, the tiny subatomic particles that orbit the nucleus of atoms. Flowing electrons produce an electrical current that can be used to run motors, create heat and light our homes.

Electricity has only been used as a commercial energy source for less than 200 years. You can find more about it on pages 72-77.

Nuclear Energy

Nuclear energy is extremely powerful, yet its source is incredibly small. Nuclear energy is released when the nucleus of an atom either breaks apart (called 'fission') or gets larger (called 'fusion').

Nuclear fusion powers stars, including our Sun, and scientists are now investigating how to use it as a green fuel on Earth. Nuclear fission is the fuel behind some nuclear bombs and nuclear power plants. For more on nuclear energy, see page 112.

Nuclear energy is used to make electricity, but unless it is properly controlled it can be very dangerous.

STUFF: THE BASICS

19

NATURE STUFF

F

Natural resources such as rocks, water, soil and air are the matter that allow living things to grow and reproduce. They also provide us with the basic building blocks for cooking, making shelters and creating thousands of cool devices.

Our most important natural source of energy is our star, the Sun. Even though the Sun is about 150,000,000 kilometres away, without it our world would be a cold, dark, barren rock drifting in space!

In this section we'll look at the natural stuff that makes everything else possible.

IT CAME FROM THE BIG BANG

We live surrounded by stuff. We ourselves are made of stuff. So, where did it all come from? Well, somewhere around 13.8 billion years ago, our universe was created in an incredibly powerful explosive event called the Big Bang.

The earliest universe – straight after the Big Bang – was so hot and dense that atoms didn't exist. Instead, there was loads of energy, including light, and there were lots of separate protons, neutrons and electrons. (Go back to page 12 for more on these subatomic particles.)

After about 380,000 years, things cooled down enough for the two simplest elements, hydrogen and helium, to form – the first atoms ever. On Earth, both of these elements exist as gases, but they are also the main ingredients of our Sun and most other stars. In fact, they are still the two most abundant elements in the universe today.

But what about the rest of the elements? How did they get here? That's where gravity comes in. Gravity is a force that pulls things together. Atoms are super tiny, but even tiny things are affected by gravity. Little by little, atoms of hydrogen and helium in the early universe started clumping together.

NATURE STUFF

23

STARS

Remember how matter can turn into energy and energy can turn into matter? Well, when the clumps of atoms got big enough, the pressure of all that matter squeezing together started converting some of the matter back into energy in a process called nuclear fusion. When big clumps of matter start creating energy like this, we call them stars.

As these first stars grew, the even more enormous pressure at their centres smushed the smaller atoms together to make heavier elements such as carbon, oxygen and iron.

After many millions of years, those first stars began to run out of elements they could convert to energy and they began to die. When this happens to large stars, gravity causes them to collapse in on themselves, heat up again, and then blow apart in a cosmic explosion called a supernova. Supernovas produce even heavier elements, which get blasted into space and form a giant cloud of dust and gas known as a nebula. That's where new stars - and their infant solar systems - are born.

BONUS!

Many of the elements found in your body, including carbon and iron, formed in the centre of ancient stars, so you really are 'star stuff'!

BIRTH OF OUR SOLAR SYSTEM

About 4.6 billion years ago in a **NEBULA** formed by the explosion of a dying star...

...a big lump of matter pulled together ever more tightly until the centre of it burst into a star and became our **SUN**.

GAS AND DUST swirled around the area further from the centre of the clump.

Slowly most of that gas and dust came together to become **PLANETS, MOONS, DWARF PLANETS, ASTEROIDS** and all of the other bodies in our Solar System.

NATURE STUFF

25

THE GROUND BENEATH US – ROCKS

When the solar system formed, some elements, such as iron, nickel, oxygen and silicon, became the rocks we have on Earth. Rocks may not seem too exciting, but they really are some awesome stuff! Not only do they make up the continents, but they are also found deep under the oceans.

With the exception of Earth's core, most of the interior of our planet is also made of rock. Here, where temperatures are much hotter, some of the rock melts to form a liquid called magma. Sometimes the magma flows out onto the surface as lava, which cools to form new rock.

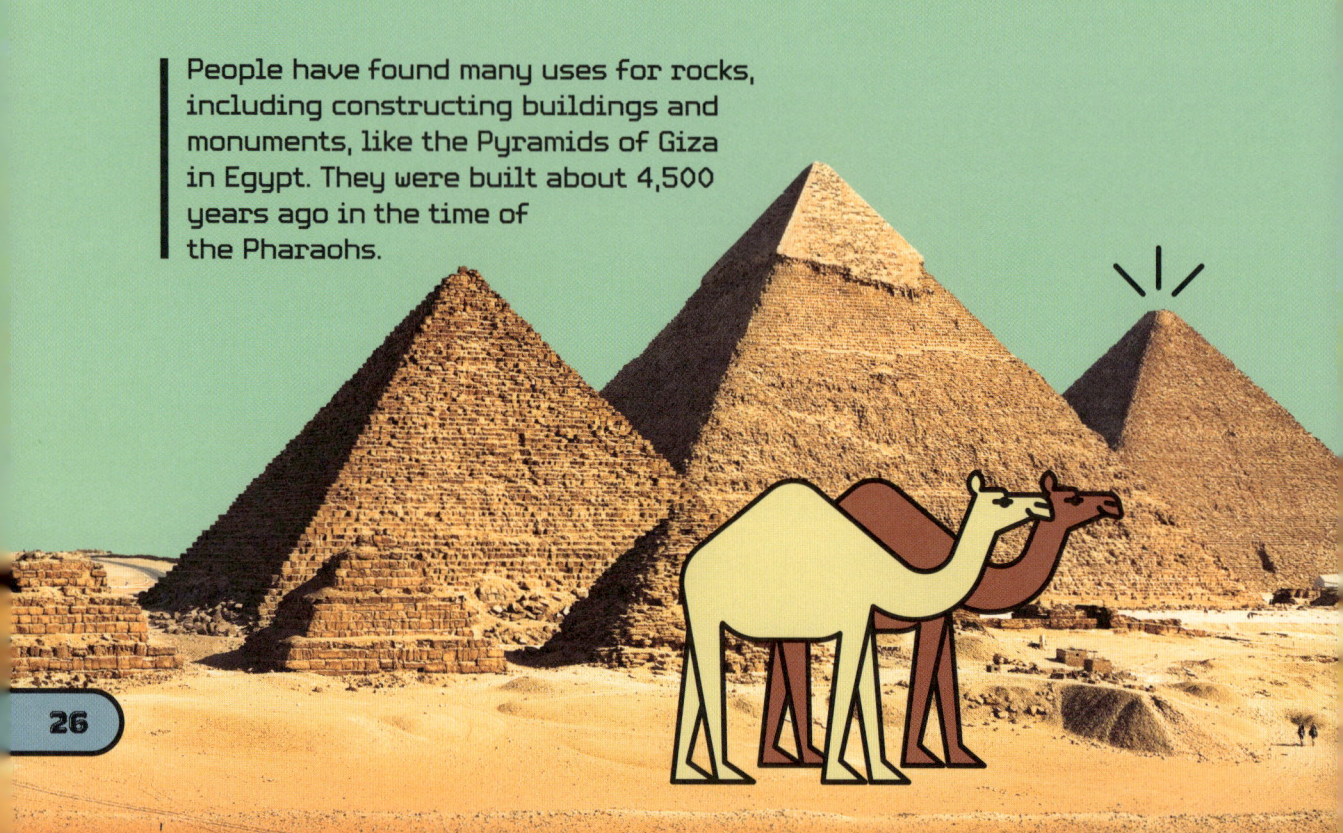

> People have found many uses for rocks, including constructing buildings and monuments, like the Pyramids of Giza in Egypt. They were built about 4,500 years ago in the time of the Pharaohs.

Most rocks are made of minerals – elements or combinations of elements that form crystals. And almost all of the metals we use come from special rocks called ores. One of my favourite minerals is halite (check out its compound on page 14). It's made of two elements, sodium and chlorine. The coolest thing about it? It's the only mineral we grind up and eat. Why don't we talk more about halite? We do, we just call it salt!

Rocks don't last forever. Water, wind and ice break them into smaller pieces called sediment. That's where we get stuff like sand and clay. Sediment also is a big part of soil (more about that on page 30).

Everywhere you look, constantly changing and sometimes even edible – you can see why rocks are high on my list of coolest stuff.

BONUS!

You can grow your own mineral crystals by taking a large plastic cup and filling it halfway with warm water. Stir in about 5 teaspoons of salt until it all dissolves. Allow the cup to sit undisturbed for about a week. As the water in the cup evaporates, you'll start to see tiny halite crystals growing on the side of the cup.

MAGNETS

Most rocks pretty much just sit there and let outside forces change them. But a small number attract other rocks. We call these oddballs lodestones, or natural magnets.

A magnet (including a lodestone) is special for two reasons – it is a type of metal that attracts iron, steel and several other metals, and it also lines itself up with other magnetic fields. Earth has a magnetic field, and a compass works because the magnetic needle in it lines itself up along Earth's magnetic field, pointing north-south.

Not every piece of iron is a magnet. How come? Well it all comes down to electrons (see page 12). When they orbit the nucleus of an atom, electrons also spin. The spinning electrons create something called a magnetic domain. In most rocks (including regular pieces of metal), electrons spin in different directions, so the domains point all over the place. When the electrons all spin in the same direction, the domains line up, and, presto, you have a magnet!

The top illustration shows magnetic domains in a regular piece of iron, and the bottom illustration shows the way they line up in a magnet.

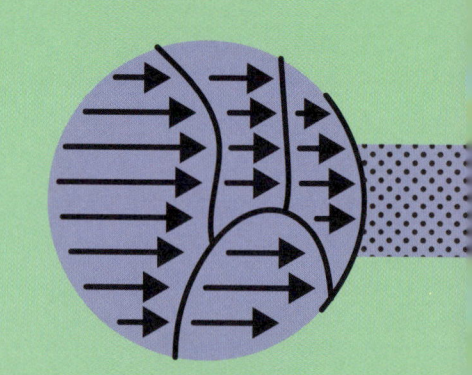

The rock below is a lodestone that has attracted small pieces of iron.

NATURE STUFF

29

YUM... DIRT

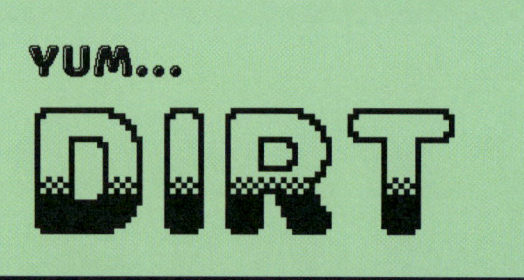

Minerals are found in rocks. They are also found in the broken-up rocks, called sediment, that make up most of the dirt on Earth's surface. Over time, pieces of sediment break down even further in a process called weathering. This releases their chemical elements. Other chemicals get into the soil from decomposing (or rotting) dead plants, animals, and fungi. This wonderful mix of stuff is called soil.

Both sets of chemicals – from dead things and from sediment – act as nutrients. These nutrients make soil the perfect home for millions of different living things, from bacteria, fungi and plants, to insects, worms and cute little bunnies. Without soil, there would be no forests, grasslands, or fields of corn or other crops. And without those environments, humans would find it hard to exist.

Most soils are made up of different layers called 'horizons'. The O-Horizon and A-Horizon contain most of the nutrients, which are used and pooped out by earthworms and other life forms found in the soil.

ORGANIC / O-HORIZON

TOPSOIL / A-HORIZON

SUBSOIL / B-HORIZON

PARENT MATERIAL / C-HORIZON

NATURE STUFF

31

AWASH IN WATER

Earth is an exceptionally wet world. About 71% of its surface is covered with liquid water. Scientists estimate that we have about 1.386 billion cubic kilometres of water on Earth, which is enough to fill over 500 trillion Olympic-sized swimming pools! Around 97% of all that water is in the oceans.

Water is very special stuff, and critical to life on Earth. Living things are made mostly of water, and most need a constant supply of water to survive.

Freshwater – ice and glaciers, lakes, rivers, ponds, streams, groundwater, water vapour, and the water in living things – makes up less than 3% of all the water in the world.

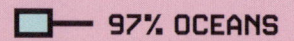

▢ — 97% OCEANS
▢ — 3% FRESHWATER

BONUS!

A little more than half the weight of an average adult person is water, but this number is even higher in children. In fact, when babies are born about 78% of their body weight comes from water!

The Wonderful Water Molecule

We met the water molecule briefly on page 15, but it deserves more attention than we gave it there. Water is a very cool chemical compound made of two hydrogen atoms and one oxygen atom bonded together. The two hydrogen atoms stick out of one end of the molecule, giving that end a positive charge. The oxygen sticks out of the other end and gives that end a negative charge. This makes water a 'polar molecule', which acts sort of like a magnet, with the oxygen (negative) end of one molecule attracted to the hydrogen (positive) end of another.

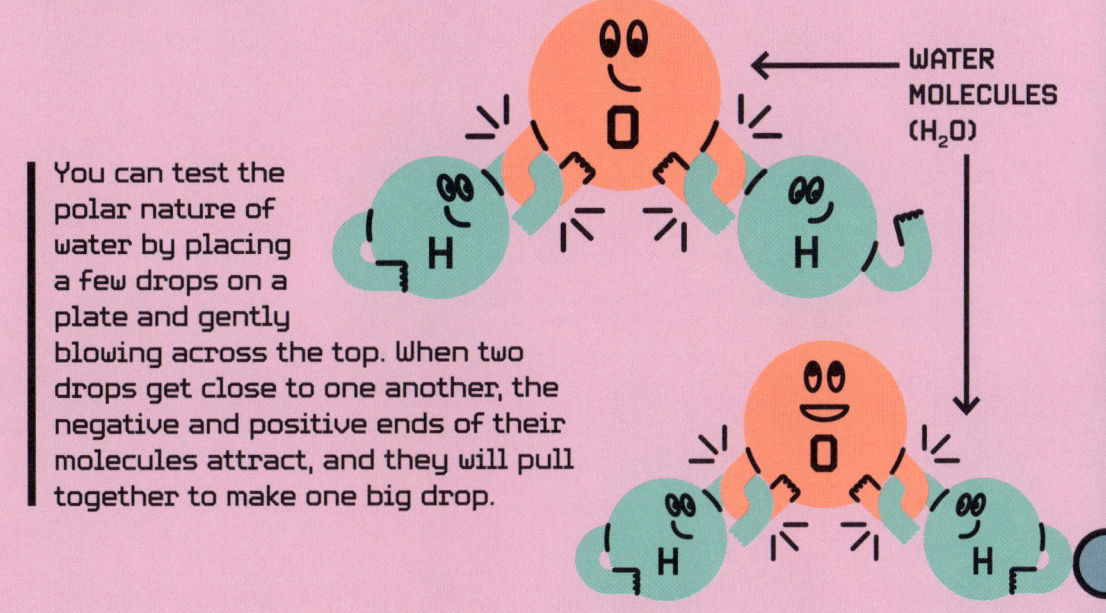

You can test the polar nature of water by placing a few drops on a plate and gently blowing across the top. When two drops get close to one another, the negative and positive ends of their molecules attract, and they will pull together to make one big drop.

← WATER MOLECULES (H_2O)

NATURE STUFF

FROZEN

Living things couldn't live without liquid water, but solid water (otherwise known as ice) is very cool stuff too! One of the most amazing things about it is the way it protects some ecosystems. You see, when water starts to freeze into ice, it expands to take up more space. That makes it less dense, and means solid ice will float on liquid water. Just look at a glass of water with ice in it. So, ponds freeze from the top down, and the ice on the surface keeps the rest of the pond from freezing solid. As a result, the animals that live in the pond can survive until the weather gets warmer and the ice melts.

RECYCLED

Most of the water on Earth has been here for billions of years, so the water you drink today could be the same water a dinosaur spit into 70 million years ago! There's no need to get grossed out though. That's because we have something called the water cycle that naturally cleans and recycles water on Earth.

When liquid water is heated by the Sun, some of it evaporates and turns into a gas called water vapour. Water vapour is pure water. The evaporation process leaves any dirt or bacteria behind. As the clean water vapour rises in the air, it cools and turns back into tiny water droplets. This is called condensation and it forms clouds. Finally, when the drops get too big, precipitation (rain, snow, sleet or hail) happens, and the water falls back to the surface. Then the cycle starts all over again!

| Imagine sharing your water with a dinosaur!

LIFE-GIVING
LIGHT

Sunlight is incredible stuff. It's all radiant energy (see page 17), but there's much more to it than the visible light we can see with our eyes. The Sun also produces radio waves, microwaves, infrared (which is often called heat), ultraviolet rays, x-rays and gamma rays. What makes these forms of radiant energy different from one another is how fast their waves are vibrating back and forth. At one end of the spectrum, radio waves vibrate the slowest. At the other end, gamma rays vibrate super fast. Taken together, these forms of radiation make up the electromagnetic spectrum.

Over the years people have discovered uses for most kinds of electromagnetic radiation. Radio waves are used for communicating and for broadcasting television and radio programs. Microwaves and infrared waves are used for cooking food. Infrared waves also help us keep warm. X-rays allow doctors to see inside our bodies, and gamma rays are used to treat cancer.

Sunlight makes almost all of life on Earth possible, including us, because plants use it to make their food, and we (and other animals) eat plants.

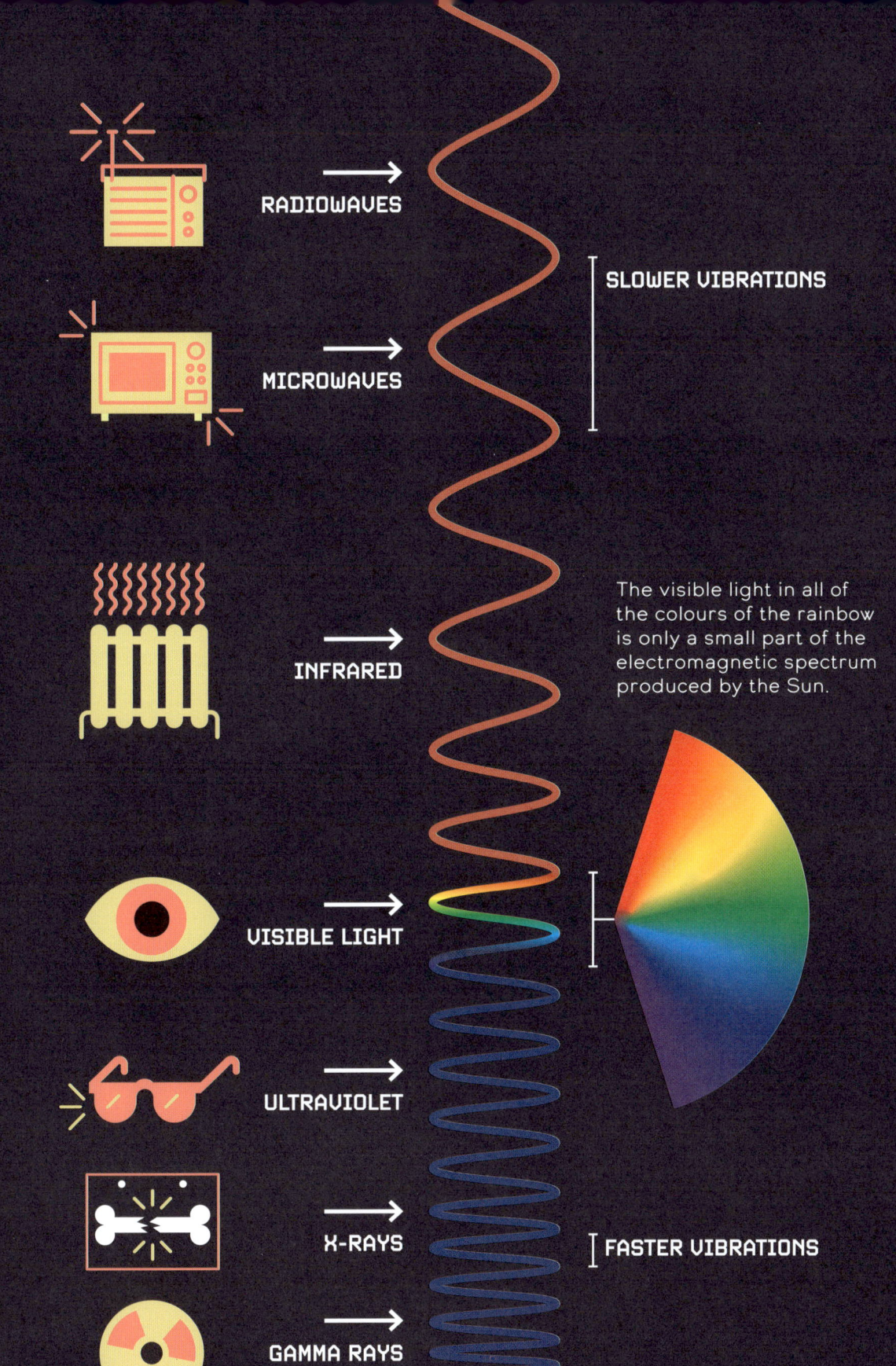

RADIOWAVES

MICROWAVES

SLOWER VIBRATIONS

INFRARED

The visible light in all of the colours of the rainbow is only a small part of the electromagnetic spectrum produced by the Sun.

VISIBLE LIGHT

ULTRAVIOLET

X-RAYS

FASTER VIBRATIONS

GAMMA RAYS

NATURE STUFF

37

WEATHER-FILLED AIR

When it comes to the stuff we need to live, air is just as important as food and water. That's because many living things here on Earth depend on the gases found in air. Plants and other life forms that carry out photosynthesis need a constant supply of carbon dioxide to make food. In the process, they release oxygen, which animals (including us humans) need to breathe. (More about photosynthesis on page 50.)

The air surrounding our Earth also controls the weather. Since the gases that make up air are a type of matter, they have mass and press down on the surface. This is called air pressure. When the temperature of the air changes, so does the air pressure. Air rushing from areas of high pressure to areas of low pressure is what we call wind!

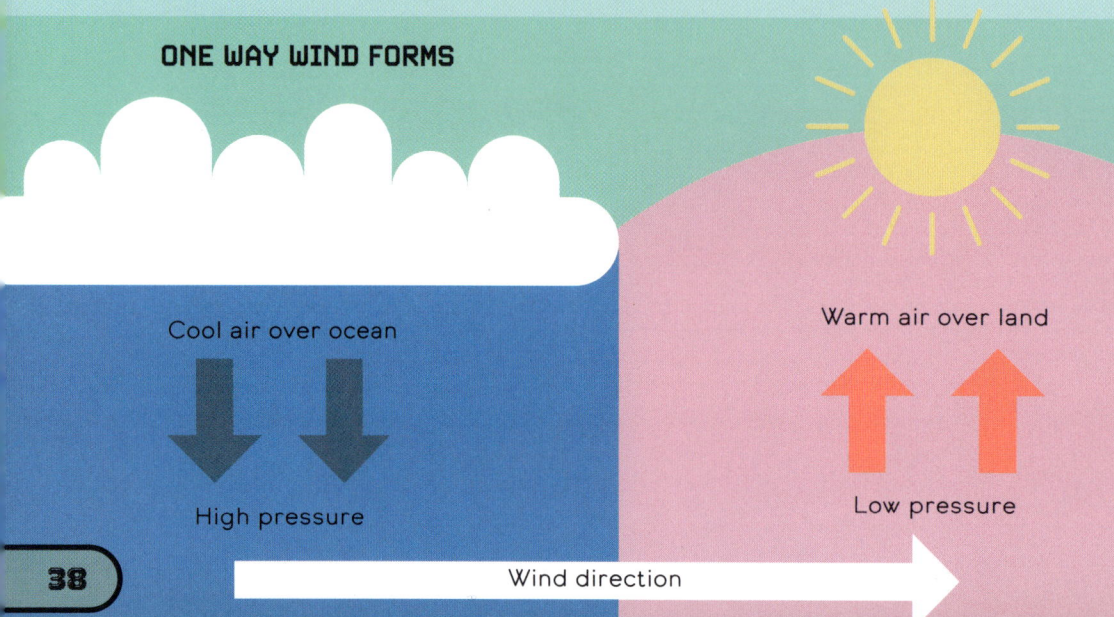

ONE WAY WIND FORMS

Cool air over ocean
High pressure

Warm air over land
Low pressure

Wind direction

Hurricanes form in the warm, tropical areas of Earth near the equator. Their super-fast spinning winds are caused by low-pressure air near the surface of the ocean moving up through the centre of the storm and cooler, higher pressure air moving in to take its place.

NATURE STUFF

OUR GREENHOUSE

When we talk about all of the air that surrounds Earth, we call it the atmosphere. The atmosphere does more than allow living things to breathe and make our local weather – it keeps Earth warm, just like a blanket keeps you warm in your bed at night.

The warmth of that blanket of air depends on how much water vapour, carbon dioxide, methane and other greenhouse gases are in the atmosphere.

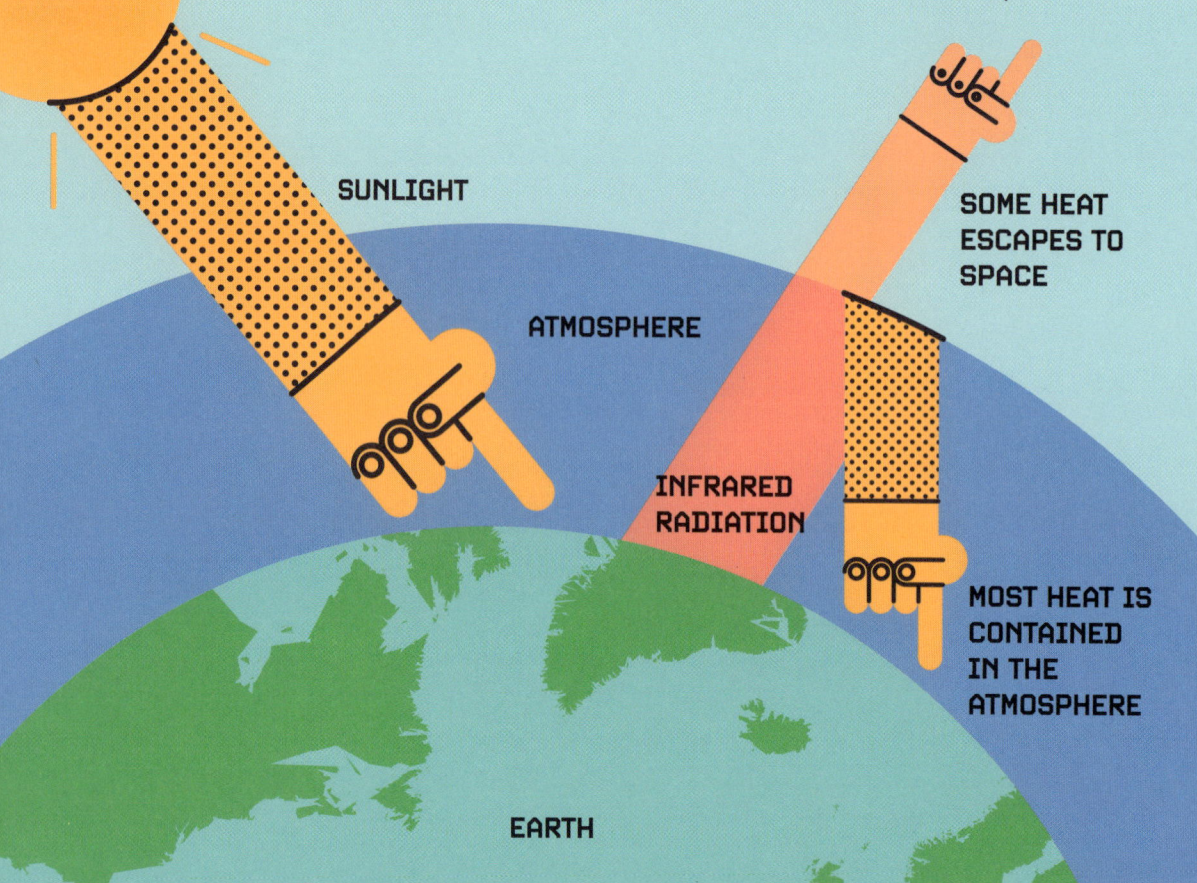

SUNLIGHT

ATMOSPHERE

SOME HEAT ESCAPES TO SPACE

INFRARED RADIATION

MOST HEAT IS CONTAINED IN THE ATMOSPHERE

EARTH

BONUS!

We worry about the greenhouse gases in the air, and for good reason. But without any greenhouse effect, Earth would be too cold for most living things to survive.

As the amount of these gases decreases, so do temperatures on Earth, sometimes to the point of causing ice ages. When the gases increase, temperatures tend to go up. For the past several million years, Earth has been at a medium temperature, the kind humans like best.

But over the past 200 years, the amount of greenhouse gases found in the air has been steadily increasing, mostly caused by humans burning fossil fuels (see page 70). The result is that our planet has been getting warmer very fast. That's what we call climate change, and it's a big problem, as I'm sure you've heard!

> When sunlight hits the atmosphere, most of the visible light passes right through and strikes Earth's surface, warming it up. This energy is released back into the air in the form of heat, also known as infrared radiation. Unlike visible light, infrared radiation can get trapped by certain gases in the atmosphere, so the air gets warmer. This is called the greenhouse effect.

NATURE STUFF

FIRE

Another thing that the atmosphere makes possible is fire. Fire is a chemical reaction called combustion. To get a fuel such as wood to burn, it must first be heated to something called the 'ignition temperature'. When this happens, molecules of gases in the fuel break apart, releasing the elements carbon and hydrogen. They link up with oxygen in the air to make other forms of matter, including carbon dioxide and water. These chemical reactions release a lot of thermal energy (see page 17), which travels out as infrared radiation, making a fire feel hot. As long as there is plenty of fuel and oxygen available, a fire will keep burning.

Most natural fires are caused by lightning. Humans, and some other animals that can start fires, probably learned from watching these natural fires.

> Lightning is caused by electrons, those negatively charged particles that whizz around the nucleus of an atom. Electrons don't always stay as part of an atom. They can build up in one place (clouds, for example), creating a strong negative charge. This is known as static electricity because the electrons are static, or standing still. If enough electrons collect, they all jump at once, or discharge, in a sudden burst, heating the air around them and turning the gases into a stream of plasma. This glowing plasma is what we call lightning, and it can be hotter than the surface of the Sun.

NATURE STUFF

THE COOLEST FEAT – LIFE

← LIFE

Our bodies (and the bodies of trees and lions and bacteria and mushrooms) are made from lots of the same stuff that makes up rocks and stars. But we are living things, and rocks and stars aren't. So, what does it mean to be alive? Well, to start with, life forms are weirdly like stars. They use energy to make matter and also break down matter to make energy. They don't need gravity to do it, though. This is the amazing feat that the very first single-celled life form came up with around 3 billion years ago, and we've been doing it ever since!

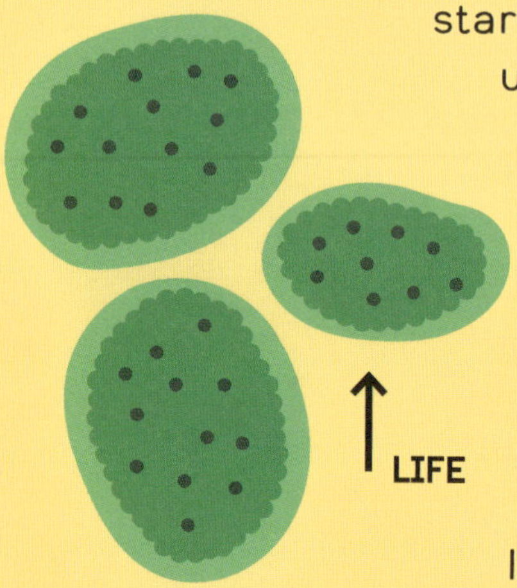

↑ LIFE

In addition to this wild feat, to count as life, something must clearly be an individual separate from its environment, and it must be able to evolve, which means to change over many generations. Living things also sense the world around them, control their own bodies, and respond to changes in their environment.

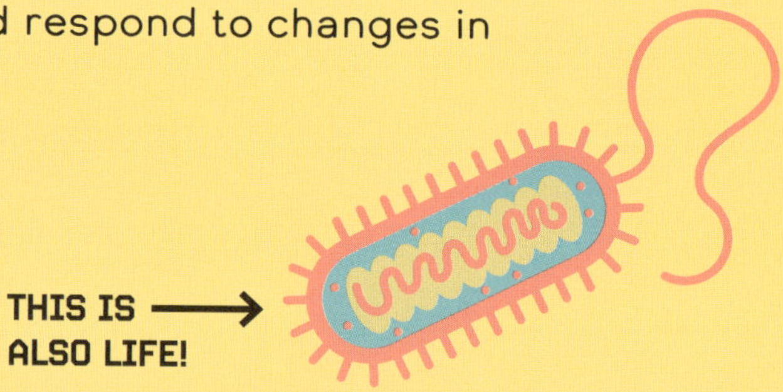

THIS IS ⟶ ALSO LIFE!

44

← THIS ONE IS LIFE TOO

LIFE ↓

LIFE →

LIFE ←

AND THIS ONE! →

← EVEN THIS ONE IS LIFE!

LIFE ↓

OOPS, NOT THIS ONE ↓

As you can see, life is enormously diverse! If you would like to find out what each of these things is, please turn to page 127.

LIFE ↓

LIFE ←

NATURE STUFF

45

DNA

From tiny bacteria to dandelions to giant blue whales, scientists estimate that there are about 9 million different species living on our world today. So, what makes you a person instead of a pine tree? The answer is some amazing stuff called deoxyribonucleic acid, or DNA for short. Every living thing has its own special DNA, which acts like an instruction manual controlling how you grow, the way the systems of your body operate, and what any children you might have will look like!

One of the cool things about DNA is its structure, a sort of long spiralling ladder called a double helix. We only know about DNA's shape because of Rosalind Franklin. In the early 1950s, she worked out how to make DNA molecules crystallise so she could take pictures of them. Her worked proved to be the breakthrough needed to build the very first model of a DNA molecule.

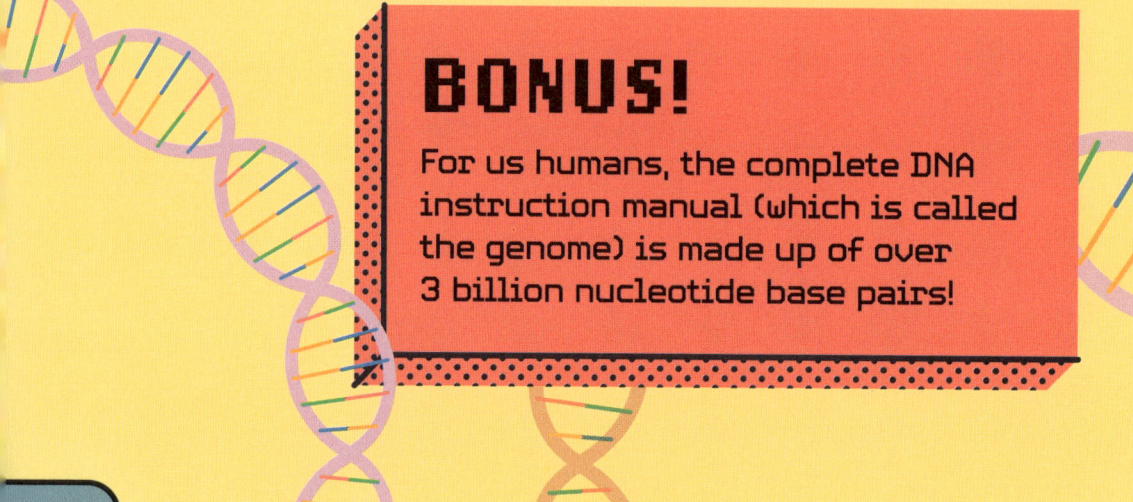

BONUS!

For us humans, the complete DNA instruction manual (which is called the genome) is made up of over 3 billion nucleotide base pairs!

A DNA STRAND

BASE PAIR

- 🟢 ⊢ ADENINE (A)
- 🔴 ⊢ THYMINE (T)
- 🔵 ⊢ GUANINE (G)
- 🟠 ⊢ CYTOSINE (C)

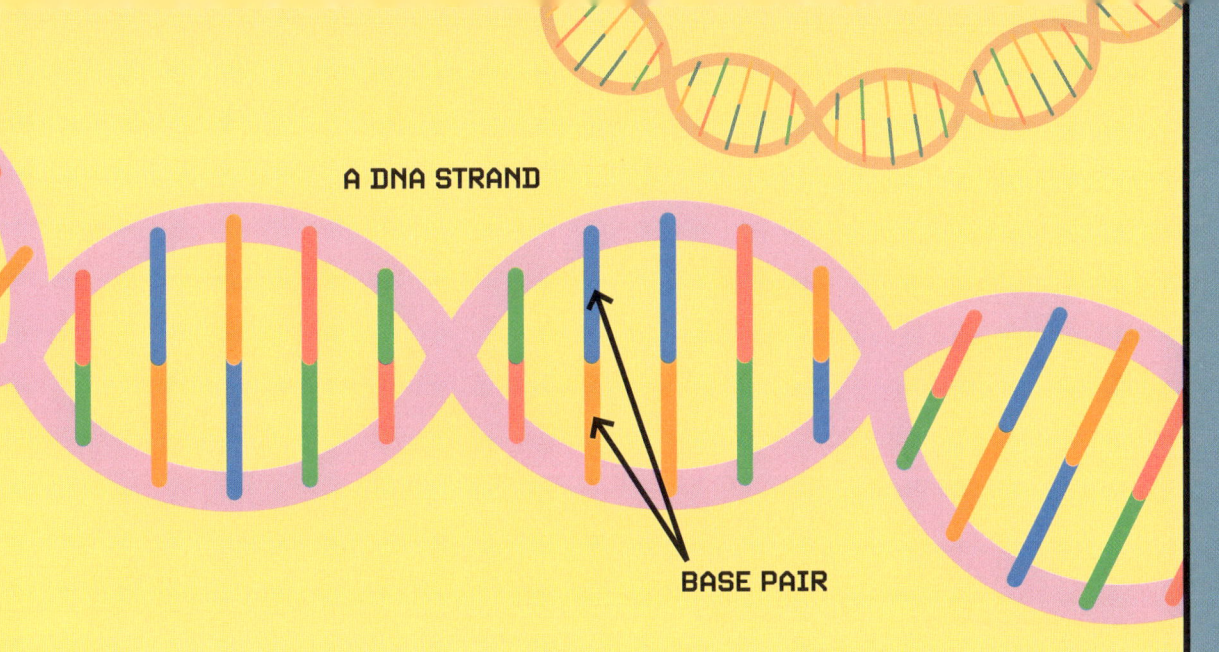

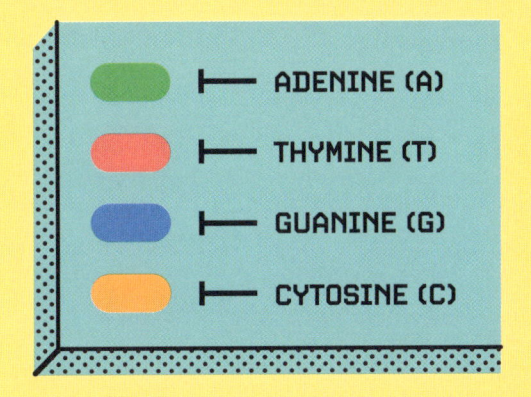

The DNA ladder is made up of smaller pieces called nucleotide bases. There are four different nucleotide bases called adenine (A), thymine (T), guanine (G) and cytosine (C). These nucleotides are linked together in pairs to make the double helix.

Just the way computer code tells a computer what to do, the order of the bases in DNA tells the body what proteins to make, and those proteins do the work of that body. Find out more about that on page 60.

Where is all of that DNA kept, you ask? Most of it is found in the nucleus of cells. Turn the page to see what those are.

NATURE STUFF

CELLS

Cells are the building blocks of life. Some life forms such as bacteria are made up of only one cell. We humans, on the other hand, can have as many as 36 trillion cells in our bodies! All cells have a few things in common. They contain a liquid called cytoplasm that is mostly water, and they are surrounded by a cell membrane that keeps their parts inside. Plant and animal cells have a few small differences, but as you can see in this diagram, they are very similar.

> About 99% of the mass of a typical cell is hydrogen, oxygen, carbon, nitrogen, sulfur and phosphorus. The other 1% includes tiny amounts of calcium, iron, potassium, iodine, sodium, zinc and several other elements. That's a lot packed into a tiny little space!

1. The **CELL MEMBRANE** separates the inside of the cell from the outside world. It is made of lipids (see page 60).
2. The **CELL WALL** only occurs in plants. It keeps the cell rigid.
3. The **NUCLEUS** is the control centre of the cell. Most of the DNA is stored here.
4. The **CYTOPLASM** is a gel-like liquid that fills the cell. Most of the other objects in the cells are suspended in the cytoplasm like fruit in jelly.
5. **MITOCHONDRIA** break down a sugar called glucose to make energy (see page 52).
6. The **ENDOPLASMIC RETICULUM** houses ribosomes, which make proteins (see page 60).
7. **RIBOSOMES** read coded instructions (mRNA) copied from DNA in the nucleus and follow them to make the body's proteins.
8. **CHLOROPLASTS** are where photosynthesis takes place in plants (see page 50).
9. The **GOLGI APPARATUS** packages up proteins and lipids for transport.
10. **VACUOLES** are spaces empty of cytoplasm that store excess water and waste products.
11. **CENTRIOLES** mostly occur in animals. They help organise the structure of the cell.
12. **LYSOSOMES** only occur in animal cells, where they break down, or digest, proteins, carbohydrates and lipids. They also digest viruses and invading bacteria.

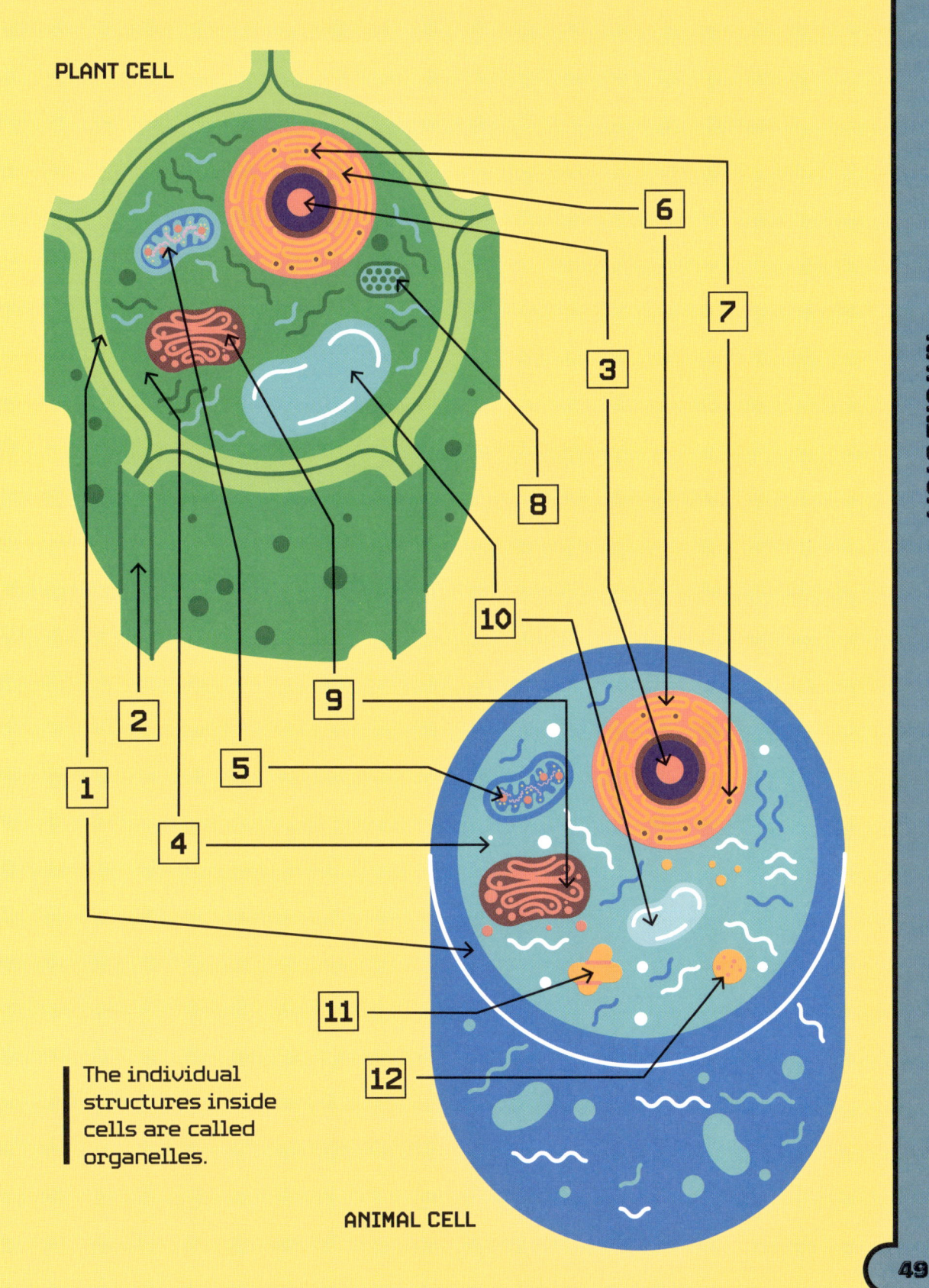

PLANT CELL

1
2
3
4
5
6
7
8
9
10
11
12

| The individual structures inside cells are called organelles.

ANIMAL CELL

NATURE STUFF

49

CHLOROPLASTS

Chloroplasts are one of my favourite kinds of stuff because almost every living thing on Earth relies on them, either in its own body or in the things it eats. On the last page we saw that a chloroplast is an organelle inside a plant cell.

Chloroplasts are like tiny factories that use the energy of sunlight to convert carbon dioxide and water into oxygen and a sugar called glucose, which the plant can store until it needs the energy. This process of using sunlight (energy) to change carbon dioxide and water into glucose is called photosynthesis.

Some scientists think that chloroplasts started out as single-celled microbes, which eventually became part of larger living things, such as plants.

> Photosynthesis seems almost magical because it makes food from stuff you find in air and water. The substance inside the chloroplast that actually absorbs the energy from sunlight is a green pigment called chlorophyll, which also gives plants their green colour. The magnified image on the opposite page shows moss cells, and the little green dots are chloroplasts.

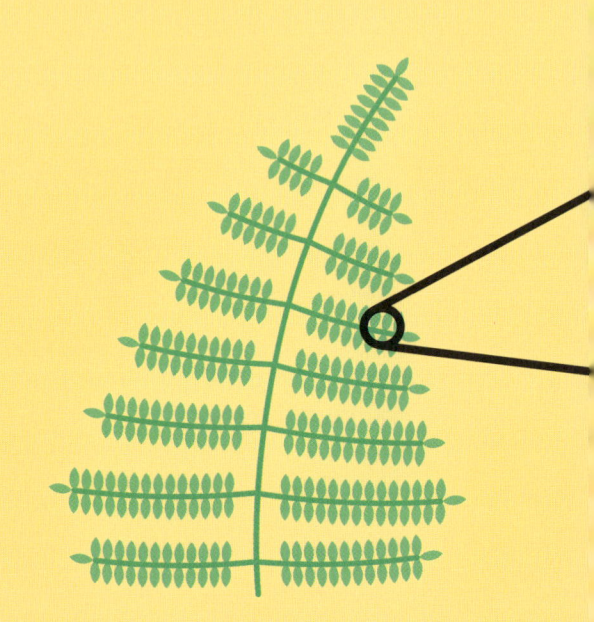

NATURE STUFF

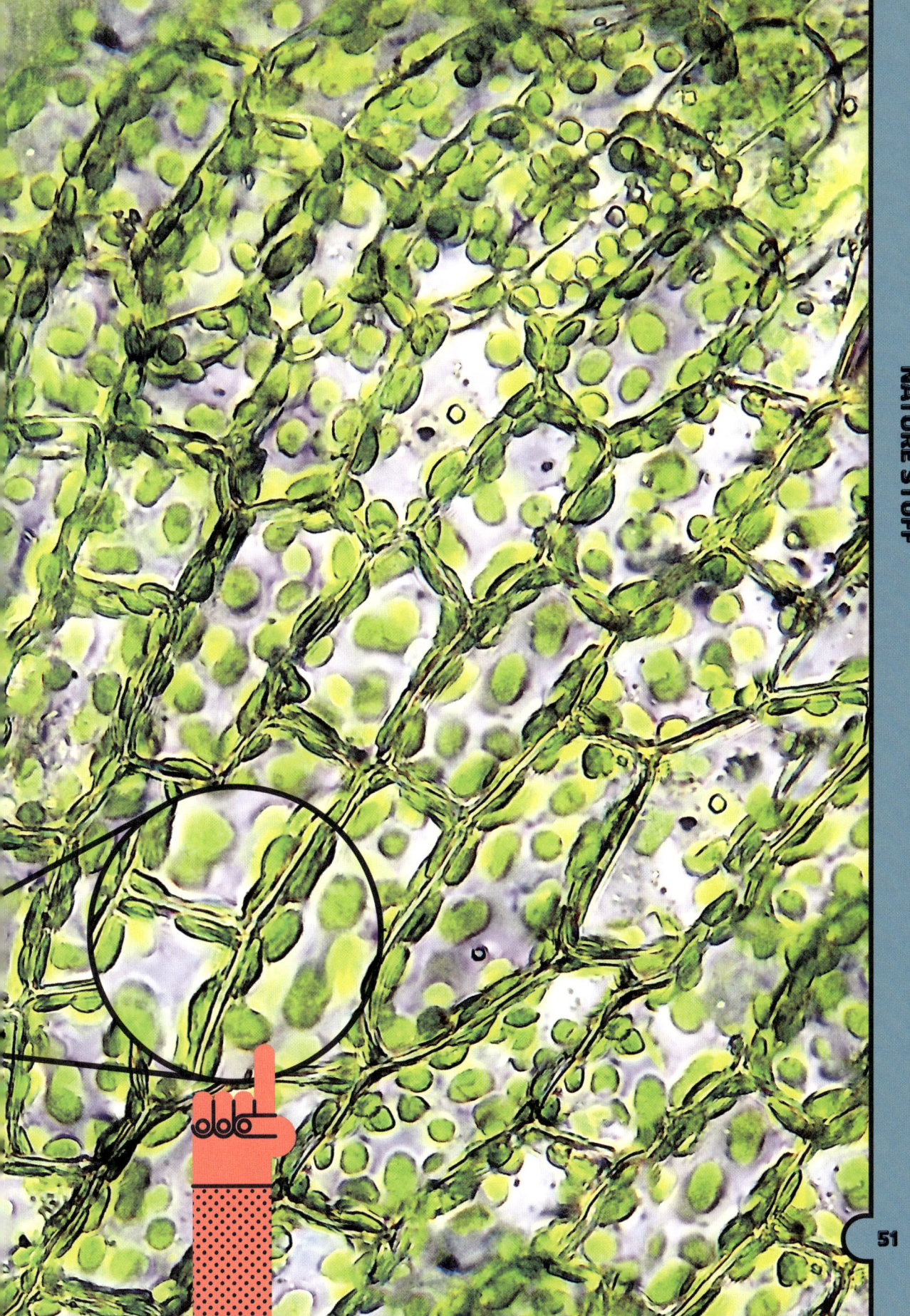

MITOCHONDRIA

Another cool cell part is the mitochondria. Like the chloroplast, it was probably once an independent microbe. It even has its own DNA!

As you now know, chloroplasts capture the energy of sunlight and use water and carbon dioxide gas to make oxygen and glucose, which stores the energy for later use. Well, mitochondria run that process backward, using oxygen to break the bonds of glucose, releasing its energy to be used when the cell needs it.

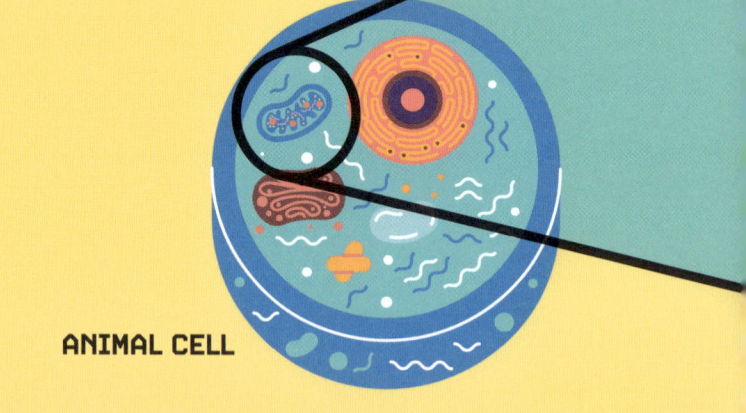

ANIMAL CELL

BONUS!

While the cell nucleus has a set of DNA from each of a person's biological parents, the mitochondria only have one set that comes from their mother!

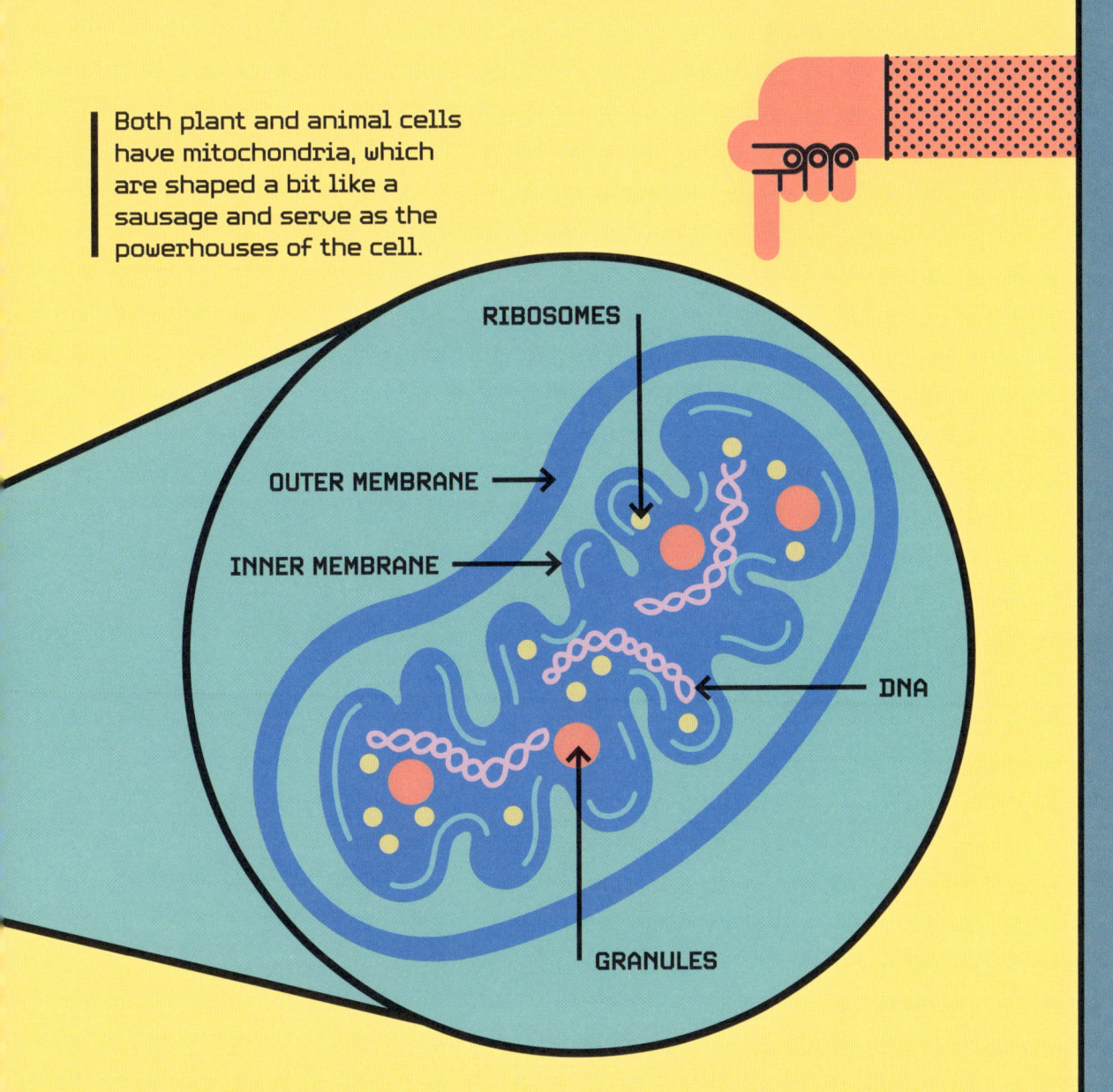

Both plant and animal cells have mitochondria, which are shaped a bit like a sausage and serve as the powerhouses of the cell.

RIBOSOMES
OUTER MEMBRANE
INNER MEMBRANE
DNA
GRANULES

The number of mitochondria found in a cell depends on the type of cell and its job. Muscle cells require a lot of energy to work, so they can have thousands of mitochondria. And some scientists estimate that the nerve cells in your brain may contain over one million mitochondria each. Red blood cells, on the other hand, usually have no mitochondria at all because they don't need to make energy. Their main function is carrying oxygen from the lungs to other cells of the body.

NATURE STUFF

MICROBES

We humans like to think of ourselves as the most important living things on the planet, but without the help of microbes our lives would come to a crashing halt! Microbes include things such as bacteria, protists, fungi and viruses, and they get their name from the fact that they are too tiny to see without a microscope.

These tiny organisms are essential players in almost every environment on Earth, including polar ice caps, hot springs and even deep ocean volcanic vents. Scientists call a community of microbes a 'microbiome', and they can be found in the air, water, dirt and even other living things, including you and me!

↑ YEAST
(A FUNGUS USED IN BREAD BAKING)

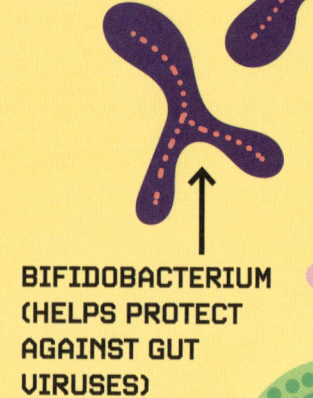

↑ LACTOCOCCUS
(USED IN CHEESE MAKING)

↑ BIFIDOBACTERIUM
(HELPS PROTECT AGAINST GUT VIRUSES)

← LACTOBACILLUS
(KEEPS OUR GUTS HEALTHY)

BONUS!

Scientists estimate that there are many more microbes in and on one single human than there are people on Earth!

Microbes in the soil help to break down organic matter and recycle nutrients so that they can be used by plants. They are also a big part of the human digestive system, helping to control how much energy you get from the food you eat. And the microbes living on your skin help to fight off infections from harmful germs. We have trillions of microbes living in and on our bodies, so many that they equal the number of our human cells.

PROTIST PHYTOPLANKTON (FOOD FOR MANY OCEAN ANIMALS) ↓

LACTOBACILLUS BIFIDUS (ANOTHER GOOD GUT BACTERIUM) →

NATURE STUFF

55

STUF

F Humans Make & Use

Humans don't just use what we find. We change it in ways that make it more useful to us. We grow, cook and process our food. We make clothing and houses to stay warm and safe. We invent methods for keeping ourselves and our surrounding environment clean. We develop medicines and other treatments to cure the sick. And we invent lots and lots of cool things to help us work faster and more efficiently, and to have fun in our free time.

In this section we'll take a close-up look at some of the stuff humans have invented to keep us living happy, healthy lives.

FABULOUS FOOD

Have you ever stopped to think about where your food comes from? It doesn't grow on supermarket shelves - I can tell you that for sure. And even though some of the food we eat is labelled 'natural', only a tiny amount of it would exist if it weren't for humans. That's why food counts as stuff that humans make.

Most of the food we eat these days is produced on some type of farm. For the past 12,000 years, people have been changing plants, animals and even some microbes to make them into healthy and tasty food for us humans.

For example, without humans there would be no corn. The ancient people of what is now Mexico liked to eat a wild plant called teosinte that grew its seeds in a small, yummy clump. Over thousands of years, farmers chose the plants with the largest clumps and saved their seeds to plant the following year. Then they did it again… and again… and again. Slowly, teosinte changed into what we know today as corn. That's why we have delicious sweetcorn, as well as popcorn and corn flour and all of the other products that are made from the corn plant.

| We eat lots of parts of plants.

Seeds
EXAMPLES: PEANUTS & PEAS

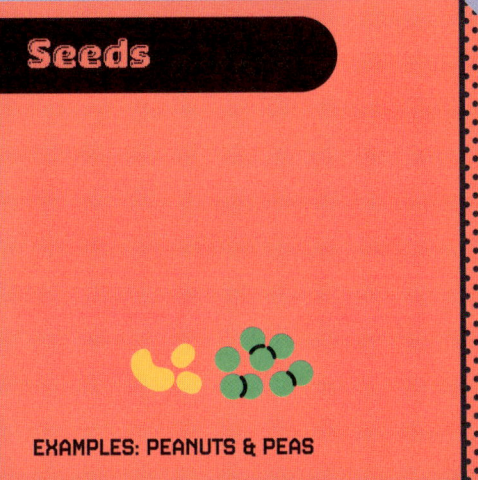

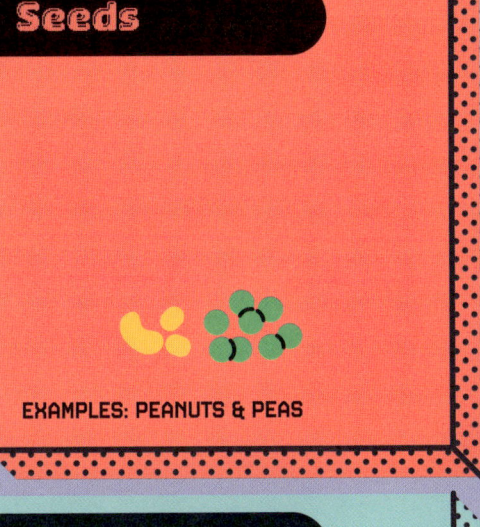

Roots
EXAMPLES: CARROTS & SWEET POTATO

Stems
EXAMPLES: CELERY & ASPARAGUS

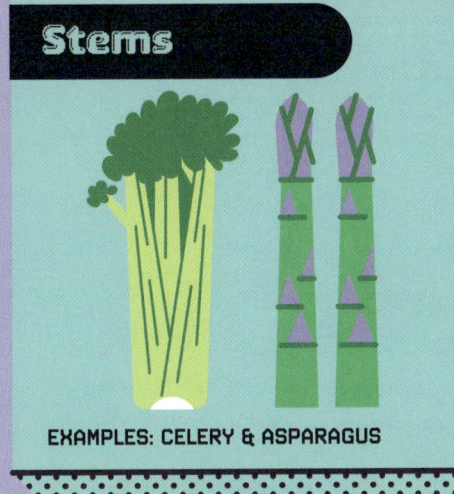

Leaves
EXAMPLES: LETTUCE & SPINACH

Flowers
EXAMPLES: CAULIFLOWER & BROCCOLI

Fruit
EXAMPLES: PUMPKIN & TOMATOES

STUFF HUMANS MAKE & USE

NUTRIENTS

To stay healthy, humans need to eat a balanced diet including several different kinds of stuff. We need macronutrients - including carbohydrates, proteins and lipids - in large amounts. We need micronutrients - vitamins and minerals - in smaller amounts. Both categories are equally important when it comes to keeping our bodies working correctly.

Proteins

Proteins are important because they are the main building blocks of our bodies. Proteins are made of smaller units called amino acids, which your body uses to build and repair bones and muscles. Some of the enzymes and hormones that help control your body are also proteins. Protein can be found in meat, fish, eggs, nuts, dairy products, beans and grains.

Lipids

Lipids include fats, oils and cholesterol. Your body needs lipids to keep cells functioning properly, and they also help your body use certain important vitamins. Your body can also break down fats to make energy.

Carbohydrates

Carbohydrates (carbs for short) are the main fuel source powering your body. They release the glucose your cells use for energy (see page 52). Simple carbohydrates include both the natural sugars found in fruit and milk and processed sugars found in sweets. Simple carbs give you a quick burst of energy. Starch and fibre, found in bread, cereal and potatoes, and also in fruits and vegetables, are complex carbohydrates made from a group of sugar molecules linked together. Starch takes longer to digest than simple sugar, providing the body with a long-term source of energy.

Vitamins & Minerals

Vitamins and minerals, such as A, C, D, iron, and calcium, are micronutrients your body needs to keep operating properly. Both vitamins and minerals do a wide range of jobs, including healing cuts, fighting infections and making bones strong. They work by helping to control the way that cells get and use nutrients from other food groups. We get most of the vitamins and minerals we need from simply eating a balanced diet that includes lots of fruits and vegetables.

STUFF HUMANS MAKE & USE

FOOD & FIRE

We still eat some of our food raw. Just think of a nice crisp apple or crunchy carrot. But nowadays much of our food is cooked before we put it into our bodies.

While it is true that fire kept early humans warm and protected them from wild beasts, it also allowed them to do something possibly even more important - cook. Some form of cooking may have started as far back as 1 to 2 million years ago. Cooking food, especially meat, was a big step forwards because it made the food easier to digest, killed bacteria on it, and in some cases added to its nutritional value.

Some scientists think that this ability to get more nutrients from food by cooking might be what made people grow bigger brains. So cooking not only makes food taste better, but it may have helped our species evolve into the creative, thinking, inventive animals we are today!

BONUS!

Whole grains are full of nutrients and energy, which cooking helps release. Plus, they contain fibre, a complex carbohydrate that your body can't digest. The fibre passes right through your system and helps you poo!

This chef in Vietnam is steaming fish for her restaurant customers.

STUFF HUMANS MAKE & USE

63

OVENS

Cooking in a modern house is fairly easy. Just turn on the stove and you have heat, pull a pot out of the cupboard and you have a container to cook in. But early cooks had to figure all this out.

The first cooks probably roasted their food over an open fire, but some of my favourite stuff appeared as they invented new ways to cook. One of those was an earth oven, sometimes called a fire pit. Around 30,000 years ago, people started digging holes in the ground and lining them with rocks. When they were ready to cook, they would place hot coals from a fire on the rocks, along with food wrapped in damp leaves. Last, they covered the pit with dirt, trapping the heat so the food would roast.

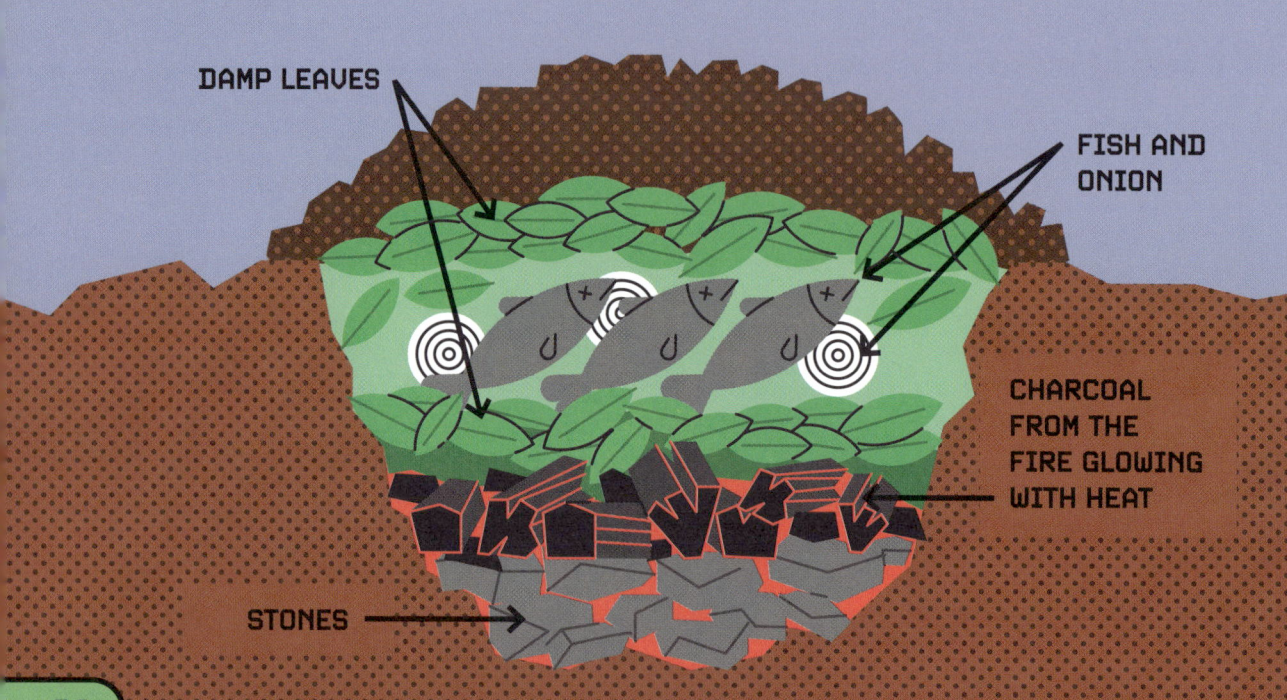

POTS & PANS

Another way to cook is to put food in boiling water. The trick here is that in order to boil something, you need to have a container that holds water and won't burn up in a fire. Pottery is a perfect solution to this problem, and cultures who invented it did a lot of boiling.

One early boiling technique that didn't require such a high level of heat resistance was stone boiling. Instead of heating the water on the fire, stones were heated and placed into the container of water along with the food. As the stones cooled down, they were replaced by new hot stones, keeping the water hot enough to cook the food. Containers made of wood and even water-tight baskets can be used for stone boiling.

Some Indigenous American cultures used baskets similar to this one for stone boiling.

PRESERVING FOOD

It's all very well to be able to grow food and cook it, but what happens when the weather makes it impossible to find fresh food? Humans have invented some pretty cool ways to preserve food when they need to make it last.

Brine

Salt mixed with water, called brine, can be used by itself or mixed with vinegar to preserve vegetables in a process called pickling. This method changes the chemistry of the food, making it difficult for harmful bacteria and mould to grow.

Brine can also be used to cause fermentation, which happens when helpful microbes in the food convert natural sugar into acid.

Tins & Jars

Nowadays, we often preserve food by sealing it in a container, but that process wasn't invented until the early 1800s. Food is placed in jars or tins and then heated in boiling water to kill any dangerous microbes that could make you ill or spoil the food. The high heat also drives air out of the container. Less oxygen makes it hard for many microbes to grow, so the food inside the sealed container doesn't spoil.

Dehydrator

Fresh food spoils because bacteria and fungi grow on it, making it unfit to eat. One simple method to combat this problem is dehydration, which basically means drying the food out. Since bacteria and fungi need water to live and grow, getting rid of the water keeps food edible longer. This process works well with meats, vegetables and fruits (think raisins). Originally people dried food by laying it out in the Sun, and some still do, but we now also have the option of a dehydrating machine.

Smoker

Meat and fish can also be preserved by smoking. This technique was probably discovered accidentally when people roasted meat over a fire, but it works better in a dedicated smoker where the smoke stays in with the food for hours. Smoking partially dries the food and it also adds chemicals that actively prevent bacteria and mould from growing. Plus many people enjoy the smoky flavour.

STUFF HUMANS MAKE & USE

REFRIGERATION

Long before people knew about microbes, they understood that storing food in a cold place helped to keep it from spoiling. Vegetables were often kept below ground in root cellars, and by the 1800s people were using ice boxes (really just insulated boxes with ice in them) to keep milk and eggs fresh longer.

Modern fridges and freezers use a substance called a refrigerant. This special stuff picks up heat from the inside of the fridge, dumps it into the room outside, then goes back to get more. The process keeps the inside of the fridge much colder than the outside.

BONUS!

The refrigeration system we use to transport and store food and other things that have to stay cold (including vaccines) includes refrigerated warehouses, trucks and ships, plus the fridges in supermarkets and in our own homes. All together, they make up what's called the 'cold chain'.

Back before refrigeration, some people were lucky enough to have ice boxes. The ice was cut from frozen lakes and ponds in winter, stacked up and covered (often with straw or sawdust) to keep it cold, then cut into blocks and delivered to homes all year long.

STUFF HUMANS MAKE & USE

FEELING FUELISH

Once people understood the value of fire for cooking and staying warm, they began testing different stuff to use as fuel to keep those fires burning. Originally, humans burned wood, grass and even dried animal poo.

Fossil Fuels

Then, by about 3,500 years ago, we started to discover other natural substances that burn well, such as coal, oil and natural gas – the main fossil fuels. Most homes, offices and factories today are heated and powered by fossil fuels directly or by electricity generated using fossil fuels.

Their name contains the word 'fossil' because they are the remains of ancient life forms that died and were quickly buried by sediments (but not the remains of dinosaurs, as some people mistakenly believe). Over time the sediments turned to rock, trapping the carbon-rich dead stuff. Heat and pressure inside the Earth chemically changed the organic matter in the dead stuff into the coal, oil and natural gas we use today.

There is no question that fossil fuels are some of the most powerful stuff on Earth, but using too much of them has gotten us humans (and the rest of Earth) into a lot of trouble. Burning them changes the carbon that has been trapped underground into carbon dioxide gas that goes into the air and adds to climate change. Plus, since most fossil fuels formed millions of years ago and not much is forming now, eventually they are going to run out.

> Much of the coal being burned today got its start as trees and other large plants in vast swamps 300 million years ago.

STUFF HUMANS MAKE & USE

ALTERNATIVE ENERGY

To replace problematic fossil fuels, scientists have developed alternative energy systems that can provide us with power without harming the atmosphere.

Wind & Water

People have long used the power of flowing water and blowing air to power mills and factories. Today, these same sources of motion energy are being used to generate electricity. Hydroelectric plants use water flowing downhill under the force of gravity to produce electricity. Wind turbines, which look like giant fans (see page 18), turn electrical generators (see page 74) as they spin.

A hydroelectric dam in the UK captures the energy of flowing water.

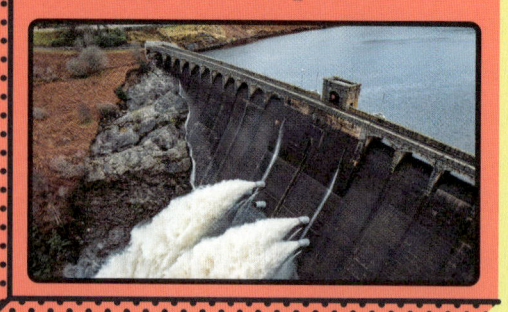

Solar panels convert sunlight to electricity on a mountain in China.

Solar

Sometimes a scientific discovery can't be used right away. One example is the photovoltaic effect. The discovery that light energy could be converted into electrical current happened in the 1800s. But those first solar cells didn't make enough electricity to be useful. Scientists kept working, and today solar cells are used all over the world.

Alcohol

We often think of alcohol as something people drink. But it has other uses, too. One is as a renewable fuel. Pure alcohol (called ethanol) is made from plants, including sugar cane, corn, and even certain grasses. Since we can keep growing these crops, alcohol won't run out the way fossil fuels will. Burning alcohol does release some carbon dioxide (because it is made from carbon-rich plants). However, when those plants are growing, they remove carbon dioxide from the air to use in their photosynthesis. All in all, alcohol fuel contributes less carbon dioxide to the air than fossil fuels do.

Brazilian sugar cane being harvested to make ethanol.

Hydrogen is already fuelling buses, like this one in Spain.

Hydrogen

Another renewable fuel source is hydrogen, the simplest chemical element. Hydrogen gas can be produced using solar and wind power to break down water molecules, which makes it a clean energy source. There is one big drawback – hydrogen has the tendency to explode, releasing its energy way too fast!

Properly controlled, it can be used just like natural gas for heating buildings and powering factories and also to fuel vehicles. Hydrogen produced by solar or wind is called a 'green' fuel because burning it doesn't give off carbon dioxide. The primary waste product is pure water.

STUFF HUMANS MAKE & USE

ELECTRICITY

One of the things we use fuel for is to make electricity - not static electricity like lightning but electrical current, the stuff that flows through the wires in our walls. Electrical current is some of the most amazing stuff in the world. Just like static electricity, it's made of electrons. But instead of standing still and then jumping wildly, these electrons flow through wires in an orderly way.

Most of the electricity that we use today is produced in power plants using a device called a generator. It is distributed to us over a network of wires running above our heads and under our streets.

Generators are very, very cool. They work based on an idea called induction, which was first discovered back in 1831 by Michael Faraday. When a magnet moves past a wire or a wire moves past a magnet, an electrical current will begin to flow through the wire.

> Simple generators use a spinning wire inside a strong magnetic field to make electricity. As long as the wire keeps moving past the magnet, electrons will keep flowing through the wire. Here's how it works: The turbine (1) is turned by steam or other energy source. It turns a shaft (2), which turns a coil of wire (3) surrounded by magnets (4). Electrons flow through the coil and out of the generator to power our devices (5).

5 TA DA! ELECTRICITY

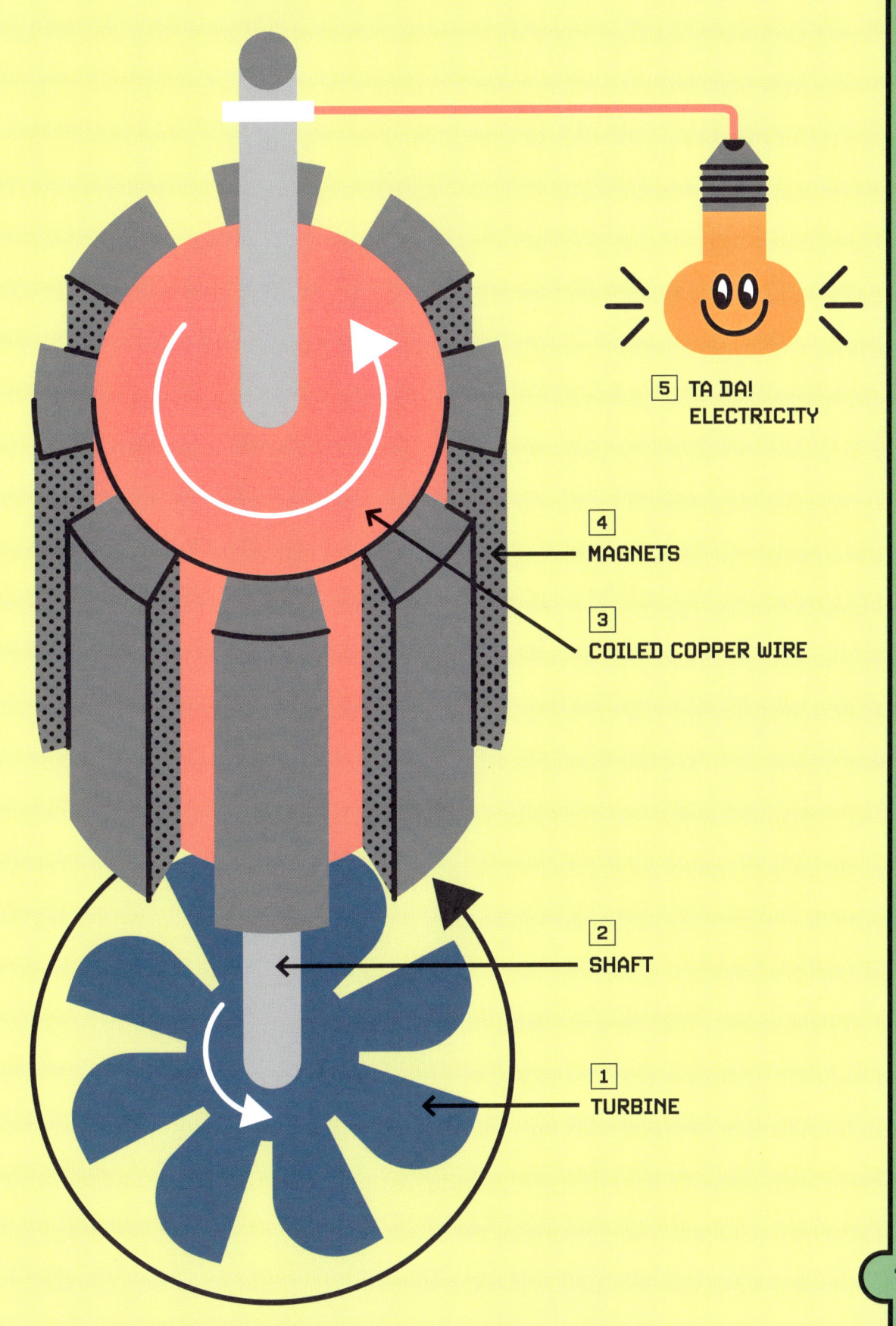

4 MAGNETS

3 COILED COPPER WIRE

2 SHAFT

1 TURBINE

STUFF HUMANS MAKE & USE

75

BATTERIES

Even before generators were invented, a clever scientist named Alessandro Volta found a way to make electrical current using chemical energy. The gizmo he built was originally called the voltaic pile, but today we call it a battery.

Electrons flow out of the negative end (called the anode) of the battery and through a wire around a loop towards the positive end (called the cathode).

The closed loop from one end of the battery to the other is called a circuit. As the electrons flow through the circuit, we capture them to power our electrical devices.

Early on, batteries were powered by simple chemical reactions using metals, such as zinc and copper, and an acid. Today, the chemical makeup of batteries is much more complex, often involving materials such as lithium, iron, phosphate, manganese and cobalt. While these new batteries are much more powerful, they still work pretty much the same way that Volta's first battery did over 200 years ago.

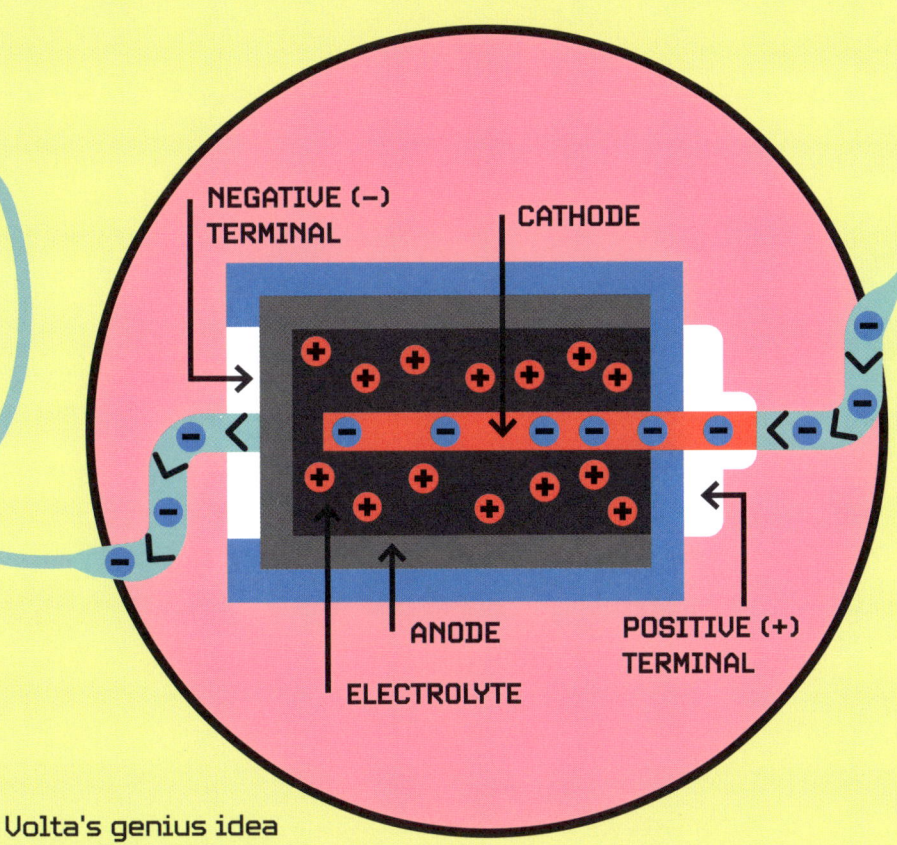

NEGATIVE (−) TERMINAL

CATHODE

ANODE

ELECTROLYTE

POSITIVE (+) TERMINAL

Volta's genius idea was to separate the anode and the cathode with an electrolyte. Originally this substance was a liquid, but in most modern batteries it's a chemical paste. The electrolyte allows ions to pass from the cathode to the anode. In the process, it causes electrons to flow out of the battery's negative terminal and through a wire, powering our devices.

BONUS!

Batteries 'wear out' when most of the available electrons have travelled from the cathode to the anode. Rechargeable batteries use another source of electricity to drive those electrons back from the anode to the cathode so they can make their trip again.

STUFF HUMANS MAKE & USE

GIVE ME SHELTER

One kind of stuff that humans have taken to great heights is shelter. Unlike many other members of the animal kingdom, humans don't have any built-in defences against the weather or against other animals that might want to turn us into dinner. Turtles, for example, grow protective shells, and hermit crabs literally carry their homes on their backs. Monkeys and birds can easily retreat to the safety of trees, moles and rabbits hide in underground burrows, and some bats shelter in caves.

At first, our human ancestors behaved a lot like those bats. Scientists have uncovered evidence that as far back as 2 million years ago, they took shelter in natural caves. But there are lots of places without good natural shelter. As people travelled, they needed other forms of housing. So, they used their big brains and skilful hands to build simple homes from the materials they could find in the environment.

Early on there was no need for permanent structures, so shelters were simple and were made from natural materials such as rocks, branches, animal skins and grass.

STUFF HUMANS MAKE & USE

79

BUILDING MATERIALS

When people began to settle in permanent villages and, later, in cities, they started inventing new building materials, and their structures really started to take shape!

Bricks

Rock was a natural choice for early builders, but stones are hard to cut and often in short supply. More than 9,000 years ago, people began making mud bricks and drying them in the Sun. These worked well in dry areas but didn't stand up well to rain. By about 5,000 years ago, people in China had discovered that heating the bricks in an oven made them much stronger. The idea spread around the world, and fired brick is still in use today.

Cement & Concrete

To build a really strong brick structure, you need something glue-like to hold the bricks together. That's where cement comes in. Over 4,500 years ago, builders in India used a mineral called gypsum to stick their bricks together. The Romans made an even stronger cement from calcium oxide, called lime. They were also the first ones to mix cement and sand to make concrete, which can be poured to make sidewalks or turned into blocks.

Iron & Steel

People had been using metals for tools and weapons for thousands of years, and over time they began using metal in buildings, too. By the late 1700s, iron was being used to build bridges and towers. But iron is heavy and can rust and break. That's where steel comes in. Technically speaking, steel is not a pure metal. Instead, it is an alloy (or mix) made from the elements iron and carbon. Steel is stronger than iron, so builders can use less, making it perfect for building extremely tall structures and super-long bridges.

Polymers

Today, builders have many new materials, most of which were created over the past century. Stuff such as plastics, resins and foams all fall under the heading of synthetic polymers. These materials are made by creating long chains of molecules using a variety of chemicals, and they have lots of different properties. Some can be bent into unusual shapes or can be sprayed on as liquids and become solid, adding strength and insulation to a building. Most of these synthetic substances are lightweight and extremely tough.

STUFF HUMANS MAKE & USE

COVER UP WITH CLOTHES

Another reason humans can live in all kinds of climates is that we protect our bodies with a whole category of cool stuff – clothing. It's hard to know what ancient people wore because clothing tends to rot away over time, but evidence points to animal skins sewn together just the way you might sew on a button today.

We still wear animal skins in the form of leather, but most of our clothing nowadays is made of woven or knitted fabric. So how did ancient people get from wearing bearskins to fabulous fabrics?

Based on the size and shape of the oldest needles, many scientists believe that the first 'threads' used to sew skins might have been tendons or ligaments from animals and vines from plants. But by around 50,000 years ago, people had begun to spin (or twist) natural plant or animal-fur fibres together into long strands. Eventually they figured out they could use this thread for more than connecting skins. They could knot, knit or weave it to make fabric.

Over time, we humans have invented a huge range of fabrics. Nowadays, almost all of the fibres we use are either farmed (such as cotton and wool) or created chemically (such as nylon and polyester).

Though most spinning these days is done by machine, some people still create their yarn by hand, carefully pulling the raw fibres and twisting them into thread.

STUFF HUMANS MAKE & USE

FIRST FABRICS

Over thousands of years, we have gradually changed the plants and animals we use for fabric just the way the ancient Mexicans changed teosinte into corn. But all of them started out wild. Here are four examples.

Harvested flax (the plant used to make linen) is left to dry in the field.

Linen

Linen is made from the fibres of the flax plant. More than 7,000 years ago, the Ancient Egyptians were already weaving it. Some special colours and weaves were reserved for rulers, but almost everyone wore it. Not only is linen easy to care for and strong, but it's also lightweight and comfortable, especially in the summer.

Cotton

Cotton is another fibre that comes from plants that our ancestors first found in the wild. Bits of cotton fabric from about 7,000 years ago have been found in Peru and Mexico. And by about 4,500 years ago, it was being produced all the way from Egypt to what is now Pakistan.

Cotton fabric is made from the fibres of the white fluffy boll that surrounds the seeds of the cotton plant.

To make wool, the animals receive a 'haircut', and the fibres are collected and spun into yarn.

Wool

Wool is animal fur or hair that people have spun into yarn. It can come from the fleece of many animals, including sheep, alpacas, llamas, goats, yaks, musk oxen, camels and even some bunnies! Wool yarn is woven or knitted into a strong fabric that keeps a person warm even when it is wet. That's why it's so great for everything from long underwear to coats and blankets. Humans have been using wool for more than 6,000 years.

Silk

Silk was first made in China more than 5,000 years ago. It is a remarkable fibre that doesn't have to be spun into thread. That's because the *Bombyx mori* caterpillar (or silkworm) does all that work. Here's how: the young caterpillar eats lots of mulberry leaves. Once it's eaten its fill (over the course of 20 to 24 days), it uses a liquid produced by its body to create one continuous thread of raw silk, which it wraps around and around itself to create a cocoon. People unwind silkworm cocoons and weave the threads into a soft, delicate fabric.

One egg-shaped cocoon is about 7.5 centimetres long and can provide over 900 metres of silk thread.

STUFF HUMANS MAKE & USE

85

SPIN THE WHEEL

Today you have lots of options when it comes to travelling. You can take a car, bus, train or plane and in just a few hours be in another city that's hundreds of miles away. Early in human history, things were very different.

If you lived near a body of water, you could take a boat. Some boats were rowed and others powered by the wind. Boats allowed people to explore the world.

When it comes to travelling on land, the coolest thing in the history of transportation is the wheel (at least in my opinion). Before the wheel, the only means of travel was walking or riding an animal such as a horse.

1
THE LJUBLJANA MARSHES WHEEL, found in Slovenia, is 5,200 years old and was probably used on a two-wheeled pushcart.

2
A WHEEL WITH SPOKES AND A METAL RIM (OR TYRE) was used for hundreds of years on all kinds of carts, chariots and wagons.

EVOLUTION OF THE WHEEL

Wheels have gone through lots of changes over the years. People first started using wheels for transportation about 5,500 years ago. Very early wheels were heavy and made of solid wood, but by 2000 BCE people were using wheels with spokes, which were lighter and stronger.

Plain wooden wheels wore out quickly, so the ancient Celts began adding an iron band, later called a 'tyre', around the outside of the rim to make the wheel last longer.

It took another two thousand years to get to the next big step. In 1888, John Dunlop created the first practical air-filled, or pneumatic, bicycle tyre out of rubber. This basic idea soon became the standard on all cars, too.

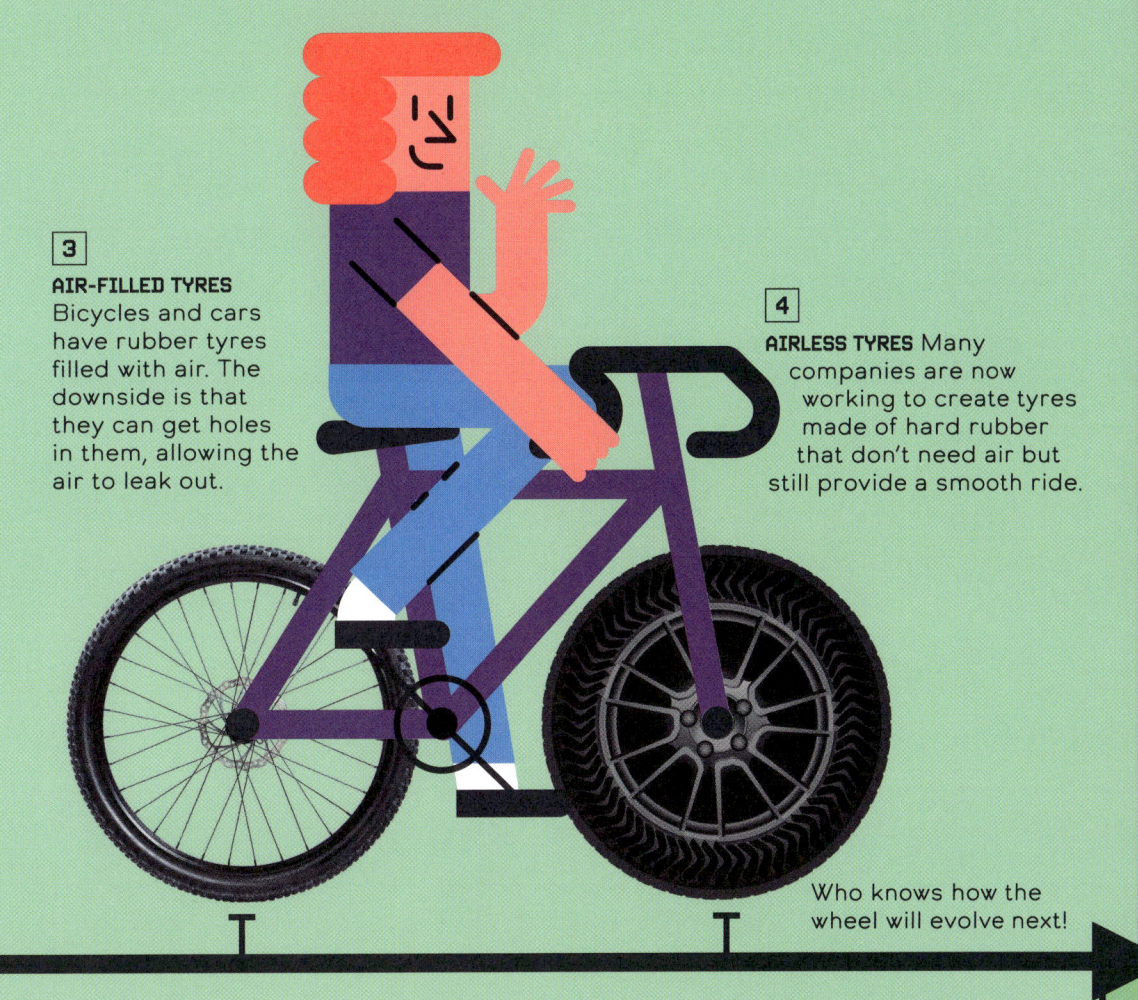

3
AIR-FILLED TYRES Bicycles and cars have rubber tyres filled with air. The downside is that they can get holes in them, allowing the air to leak out.

4
AIRLESS TYRES Many companies are now working to create tyres made of hard rubber that don't need air but still provide a smooth ride.

Who knows how the wheel will evolve next!

STUFF HUMANS MAKE & USE

MOTORS

Fire had long been used for cooking and heating, but it took until the late 1700s for people to figure out how to use it for transportation. The first vehicles to carry fires in them were steam-powered boats. Then came steam-powered trains. But the biggest breakthrough in the use of fire for transportation was the internal combustion engine – the one used to power cars and lorries that burn petrol and diesel fuel.

Steam Engine

People had been making steam for thousands of years just by boiling water. But in the early 1700s, engineers discovered ways to capture it in order to push a device called a piston, which would power a machine. Within 100 years, steamboats were chugging up and down rivers without the need for wind, and only a few decades later, railways with steam-powered trains stretched across continents.

> In 1802, Richard Trevithick developed the first steam locomotive, but the first passenger railway came in 1829 with George Stephenson's 'Rocket' (below).

The internal combustion engine in the 1903 Wright Flyer was lightweight but powerful enough to get the plane off the ground.

Internal Combustion Engine

Because they were big and heavy, steam engines were impractical for smaller vehicles. The problem was solved by the design of the internal combustion engine. It works by compressing a flammable gas in a cylinder and then igniting it. When the fuel explodes, the expanding gases push a piston that turns the wheels. These smaller, lighter engines were perfect for cars. Things really took off in 1903 when the Wright Brothers used one to power their first aeroplane.

Electric Motors

Electric vehicles are not a new idea. They date back to the 1830s, and the first rechargeable battery was invented in 1859. But they were slower, more expensive and couldn't travel as far as petrol-powered cars.

Today, electric vehicles (EVs) are giving petrol-powered vehicles a run for their money. One big reason is the development of smaller, more powerful batteries, which have brought the cost of some EVs down to compete with petrol-powered cars.

Inventor Thomas Edison (standing) worked to improve electric car batteries in the early 1900s. But his batteries couldn't propel a car as far, as fast or as cheaply as the petrol-powered engines of the time.

STUFF HUMANS MAKE & USE

89

THE WRITE STUFF – PAPER

I'm a writer, so of course I think books are great stuff. They carry stories and information far and wide. They can be shared. And they never run out of power. But without paper, books as we know them would probably not exist. So, of course, paper is one of my favourite kinds of stuff, too.

The first written works were carved into stone or pressed into clay. But stone and clay were hard to transport and store. Around 3000 BCE, Egyptian scribes developed a way to turn a reed called papyrus into a lightweight, flexible writing material that was used for more than 3,000 years.

1
Trees are cut down. Some are from special forests grown for the purpose, with new trees planted to replace those cut down.

2
The trees are cut up into logs and taken to the paper mill.

3
The bark is removed from the logs, and the barkless logs are broken into tiny chips by a chipping machine.

THE MODERN PAPER-MAKING PROCESS

During that same period, people elsewhere wrote on silk, linen, wood, and other materials. But none of them were cheap, sturdy, or portable enough to make books available to more than a very few people.

Then the Chinese invented paper. According to legend, in 105 CE a court official named Ts'ai Lun mixed tree bark and hemp fibres from rags and fishnets into a big pot of water and mashed it into a pulp. He spread the pulp over a fine screen and dried it in the Sun. The first paper was created.

Papermaking spread throughout Asia and Europe. By the 1300s paper had pretty much replaced all of those other writing materials. It arrived in the Americas with European colonisers in the early 1500s and eventually replaced the record-keeping methods practiced there. It is still the most popular stuff to write on today!

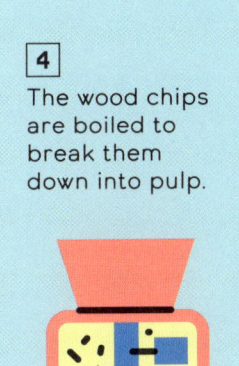

4 The wood chips are boiled to break them down into pulp.

5 Chemicals are added to clean the pulp and whiten it. Sometimes dye is added to make coloured paper.

6 The pulp is pressed onto a flat screen, and the water is squeezed out. The paper is then dried, put on huge rolls and shipped to whoever needs it, like the printing company that printed this book.

STUFF HUMANS MAKE & USE

TYPE

Paper was a huge step forward, but even with readily available paper, each copy of a book had to be written out by hand, word by word! If people wanted more books, they needed a better way to copy them. Artists in China came up with an idea. They carved each book page into a block of wood, covered the carved wood with ink, and then pressed it into a piece of paper. Those were the first printed pages.

To speed up the process, a Chinese printer called Bi Sheng made individual characters out of hardened clay, which could be arranged in different ways in an iron tray filled with sticky wax. When he wanted to print a new document, he heated the wax and rearranged the characters, or type.

> One big breakthrough in printing was the invention of moveable type. This photo shows a typesetter choosing the letters needed to spell out the text they are printing.

THE PRINTING PRESS

Using type for printing was a great idea, but it took a German inventor named Johannes Gutenberg to make it efficient. Gutenberg created a special metal type strong enough to be used over and over without wearing out. He invented a new oil-based ink that would stick to the type but also transfer to the paper without smudging. And he developed a machine that made the work of pressing the type-covered plate onto the paper quick and easy.

All the pieces came together by 1450. With Gutenberg's press, a printer could print hundreds of books in a matter of weeks, making them inexpensive enough for regular people to afford. And that's why you're reading this book right now. Pretty good stuff, eh?

> Modern printing presses use digital methods to set the type, but they are still very similar to this one of Gutenberg's, which was based on the press used to squeeze juice out of grapes.

STUFF HUMANS MAKE & USE

HERE'S TO YOUR HEALTH!

Now that we've explored food, shelter, clothing, transportation and books, it's time to explore stuff that we use to live longer, healthier lives than our ancestors could ever have imagined.

Soap

I love soap. I know that sounds silly, but think for a minute how much harder life would be without this simple cleaning chemical.

Most historians credit the ancient Sumerians from what is now Iraq with making the first cleaning agents. Over 4,500 years ago, they discovered that boiling plant ashes with fat created an amazing substance. If you rubbed it on your dirty hands or clothes or dinner plate then rinsed whatever it was with water, the dirt would come right off. But how?

Soap molecules have two very different ends. The hydrophilic end is attracted to water. The hydrophobic end is attracted to oil and dirt. The dirt-loving ends of soap molecules grab onto the dirt, surrounding each bit to make a bubble-like blob called a micelle. Then the water-loving ends grab onto the water, which washes the micelle (and the dirt it is carrying) away.

Soap's special structure does more than trap oil and dirt. It also breaks the attraction between water molecules (see page 33), which allows it to get into all the tiny nooks and crannies of whatever it's washing.

HYDROPHYLIC HEAD Loves water but does not like oil or dirt!

HYDROPHOBIC TAIL Does not like water but loves oil and dirt!

OIL

MICELLE

DIRT

DIRT

DIRT

OIL

BONUS!

The basic chemistry of soap hasn't changed in over 4,500 years.

STUFF HUMANS MAKE & USE

95

DISINFECTANTS

These days we know all about microbes, both the helpful ones we talked about on page 54 and those that can make us ill. But this knowledge is quite new. Before the microscope was invented in 1590, people didn't even know these teeny-tiny living things existed, and it took even longer to realize that they could cause problems.

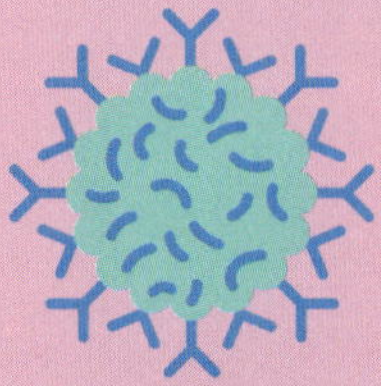

In 1865 an English doctor called Joseph Lister revolutionised surgery by introducing a procedure called 'antisepsis'. Sepsis was an infection that killed about half the patients who had an arm or leg amputated. Back then doctors rarely washed their hands or cleaned their instruments. They didn't see the point.

↑ MEASLES VIRUS

Lister understood that microbes in the air could cause food to go off, so he guessed that they might also cause sepsis. He experimented with having doctors and nurses wash their hands, their instruments and the patients' wounds with germ-killing carbolic acid before surgery.

COVID-19 VIRUS ↓

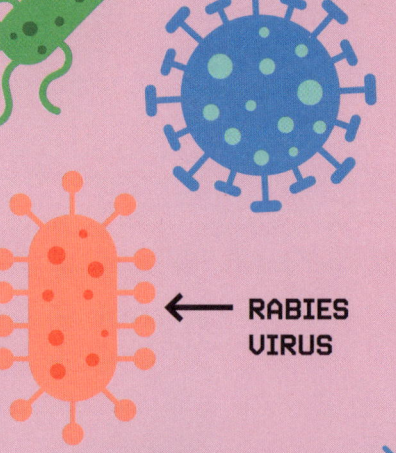

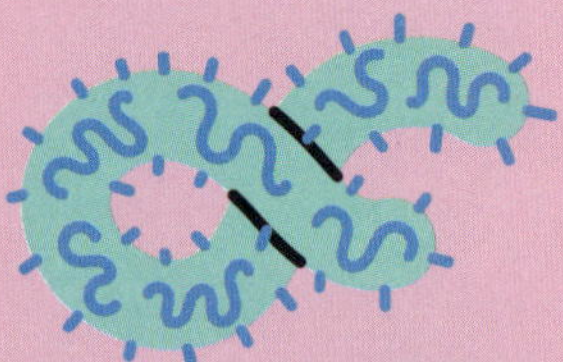

← EBOLA VIRUS

← RABIES VIRUS

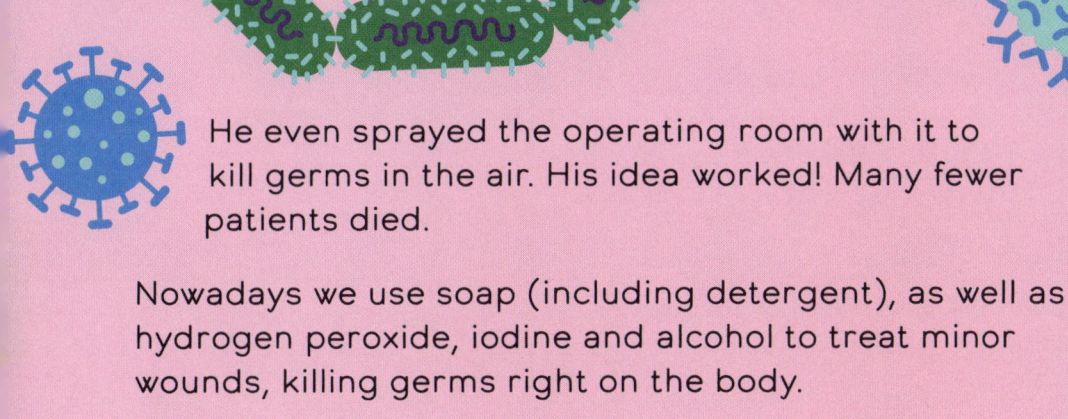

He even sprayed the operating room with it to kill germs in the air. His idea worked! Many fewer patients died.

Nowadays we use soap (including detergent), as well as hydrogen peroxide, iodine and alcohol to treat minor wounds, killing germs right on the body.

We also use disinfectant chemicals on surfaces, sprayed in the air, or even added to drinking water to kill disease-causing germs in the environment.

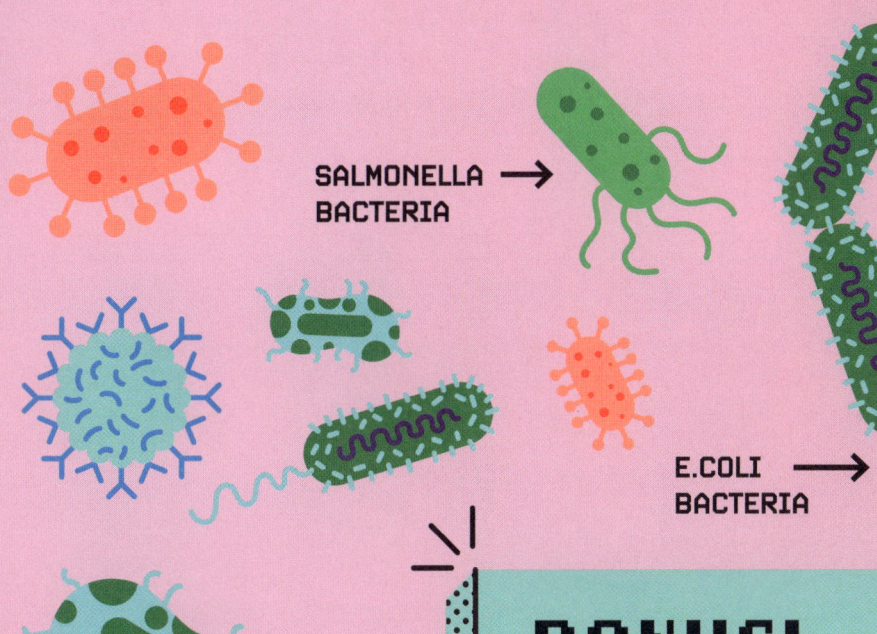

SALMONELLA BACTERIA →

E.COLI BACTERIA →

↑ BACILLUS BACTERIA

BONUS!

Tooth decay is caused by bacteria. Scientist Ruth Ella Moore helped figure that out in the mid-1900s.

STUFF HUMANS MAKE & USE

GERM FIGHTERS

Germs are all around us, so even with lots of cleaning and disinfecting, they can still make us ill. That's when science comes to the rescue with medicines that fight the diseases germs cause, and vaccines that train our immune systems to attack the germs before they have time to make us ill.

Antibiotics

When an infection is caused by bacteria, you can take an antibiotic to kill or slow the germs.

The first commercially produced antibiotic was penicillin, made from a type of mould found back in 1928. Since that time, scientists have developed dozens of different antibiotics.

Antivirals

Antibiotics don't work on viruses, and most sicknesses out there are viral. There are more than 200 different common cold viruses, for example. If you become ill from a more dangerous virus, your doctor may give you an antiviral, a medicine that stops the virus from using your cells to make new copies of itself.

Vaccines

One way to keep a virus (and some bacteria) from making you ill is to get a vaccine. A vaccine trains your body's immune system to recognise a certain type of germ and attack it as soon as it enters your body. They are usually delivered by an injection, or shot, but some come as pills or even nasal sprays.

There are several types of vaccine. The most successful Covid-19 vaccines are a particular type that uses mRNA molecules, the same stuff that translates DNA into the instructions used to build and run your body.

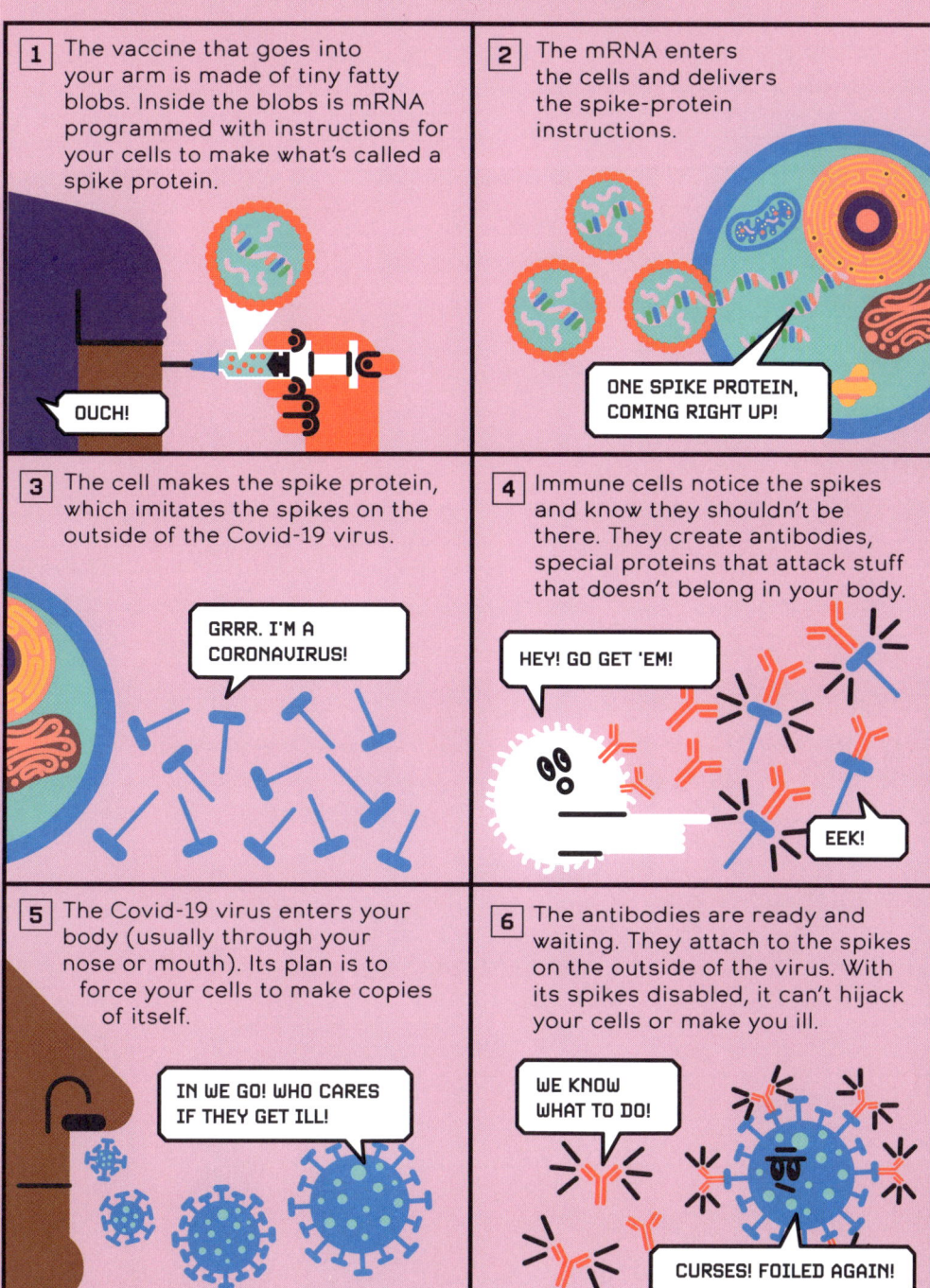

1 The vaccine that goes into your arm is made of tiny fatty blobs. Inside the blobs is mRNA programmed with instructions for your cells to make what's called a spike protein.

OUCH!

2 The mRNA enters the cells and delivers the spike-protein instructions.

ONE SPIKE PROTEIN, COMING RIGHT UP!

3 The cell makes the spike protein, which imitates the spikes on the outside of the Covid-19 virus.

GRRR. I'M A CORONAVIRUS!

4 Immune cells notice the spikes and know they shouldn't be there. They create antibodies, special proteins that attack stuff that doesn't belong in your body.

HEY! GO GET 'EM!

EEK!

5 The Covid-19 virus enters your body (usually through your nose or mouth). Its plan is to force your cells to make copies of itself.

IN WE GO! WHO CARES IF THEY GET ILL!

6 The antibodies are ready and waiting. They attach to the spikes on the outside of the virus. With its spikes disabled, it can't hijack your cells or make you ill.

WE KNOW WHAT TO DO!

CURSES! FOILED AGAIN!

STUFF HUMANS MAKE & USE

99

PAINKILLERS

Some illnesses we can cure or prevent, but many we just have to live through. That's where analgesics come in. They help lower a fever and ease the pain of sore throats, headaches, muscle aches and injuries. One of the first of these wonder drugs was salicylic acid, which was first made from a substance in willow tree bark.

People have chewed willow bark, made tea out of it, and used it as a compress for thousands of years, but it can have dangerous side effects like stomach bleeding and vomiting. Then, in 1897, the Bayer Company in Germany began producing a related substance called acetylsalicylic acid, better known as aspirin! Lots of similar drugs have been invented since, including acetaminophen and ibuprofen.

Some kinds of pain (such as having surgery) are too severe for analgesics. Luckily, anaesthesia can come to the rescue! When you are having a minor procedure, such as getting stitches or having a cavity filled, all you need is a local anaesthetic, which is usually a cream or injection. These numb a small area of the body by blocking nerves from sending signals to the brain.

General anaesthesia is used when a person is having major surgery. It makes you unconscious, so you don't feel pain or any other sensations. You can see why painkillers are pretty important stuff.

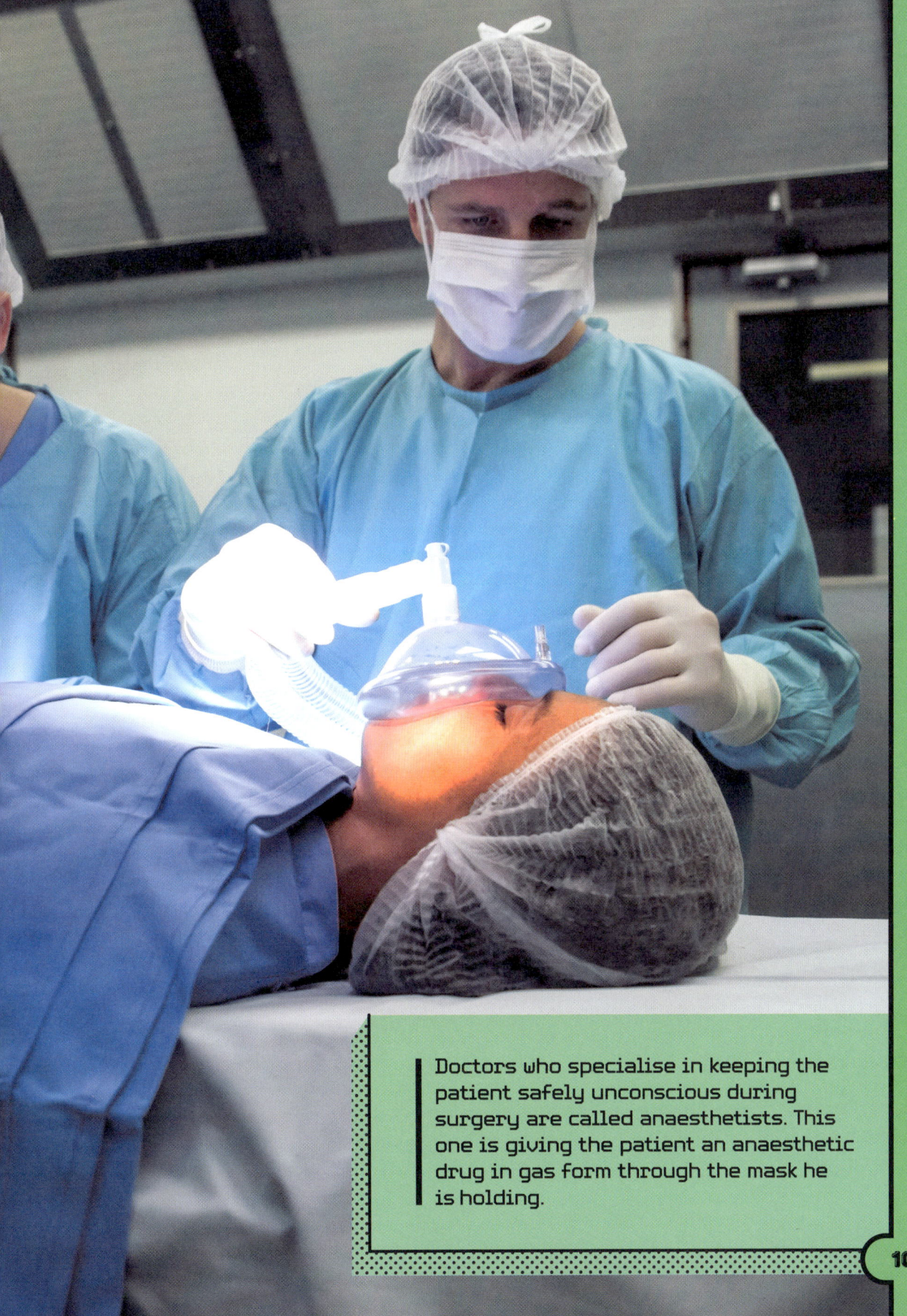

Doctors who specialise in keeping the patient safely unconscious during surgery are called anaesthetists. This one is giving the patient an anaesthetic drug in gas form through the mask he is holding.

STUFF HUMANS MAKE & USE

REPLACEMENT BODY PARTS

The human body is an incredible natural machine, but as with any machine, parts can wear out. Over the years, scientists and engineers have developed a whole host of devices that help keep our bodies running. We now have machines that can cleanse our blood like a kidney, breathe for us like lungs, and even pump our blood like a heart.

Many of these life-changing inventions have been made possible by new materials, such as ultra-strong, light, waterproof Kevlar. It was invented by chemist Stephanie Kwolek in 1965.

Here are a few of these works of biomedical engineering that have helped people live longer and more productive lives.

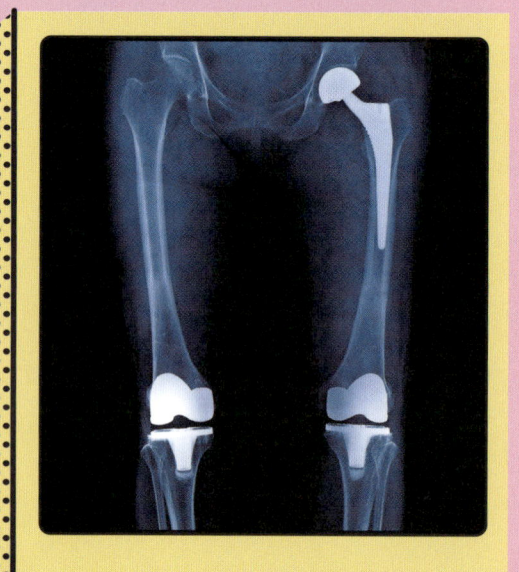

Replacement Joints

Our bodies undergo a lot of physical stress as we age, especially if we move a lot. Sometimes parts will simply break down over time, causing lots of pain. This is especially true for the joints found in your knees and hips. But thanks to amazing medical technology, some of our joints can be replaced, putting an end to pain and allowing the person to keep moving. (I have a replacement joint myself!)

Prosthetics

A prosthesis is an artificial body part that can be used to replace one missing from birth, or lost due to an accident or injury. In recent years, the development of prosthetic limbs such as arms, hands and legs has helped thousands of people.

Because of developments in computers and batteries, some of these replacement devices can even move and sense the world much like actual human parts.

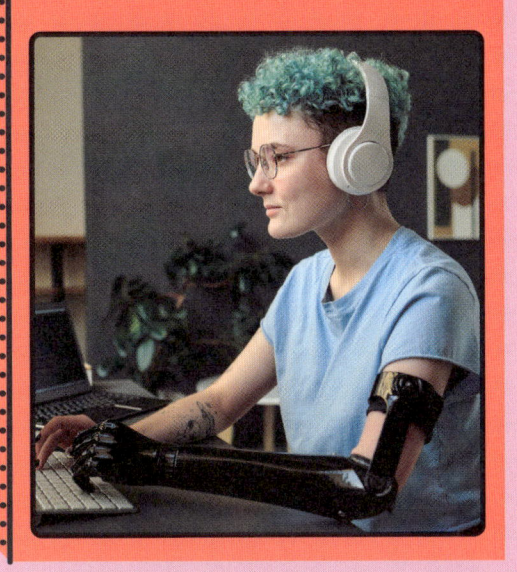

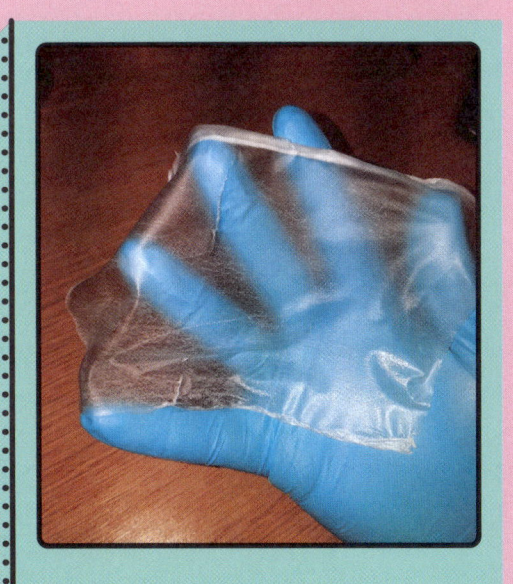

Artificial Skin

For thousands of years doctors have been trying to come up with ways to replace the skin of people who have been severely burned. Up until a short time ago, the only reliable method was to do a skin graft of actual skin from another part of the body. But recently, inventors have developed artificial skin made from a combination of living cells and synthetic polymers. Research is currently underway to use 3D printers to make 100% synthetic skin in the near future.

STUFF HUMANS MAKE & USE

103

LIGHTS, CAMERA, SMARTPHONE!

No book about stuff would be complete without the devices that make our modern lives possible, and the smartphone is the coolest of them all.

A computer (and a smartphone is really a computer) is basically a versatile problem-solving machine. It combines hardware (the physical stuff it's made of) with software (instructions that tell the hardware how to solve different kinds of problems).

The brain of a computer is called an integrated circuit, or computer chip. These bits of silicon have electrical circuits and other microscopic components etched into them. They are so small that one the size of your thumbnail can hold more than 500,000 components.

Software translates everything we put into a computer (taps on a keyboard, swipes of a screen, pictures, sound, video) into a string of 0s and 1s before doing anything with it. When the task we've asked for is done, the software translates it back into words, sounds and pictures. All of this happens so fast that we hardly notice the time it takes.

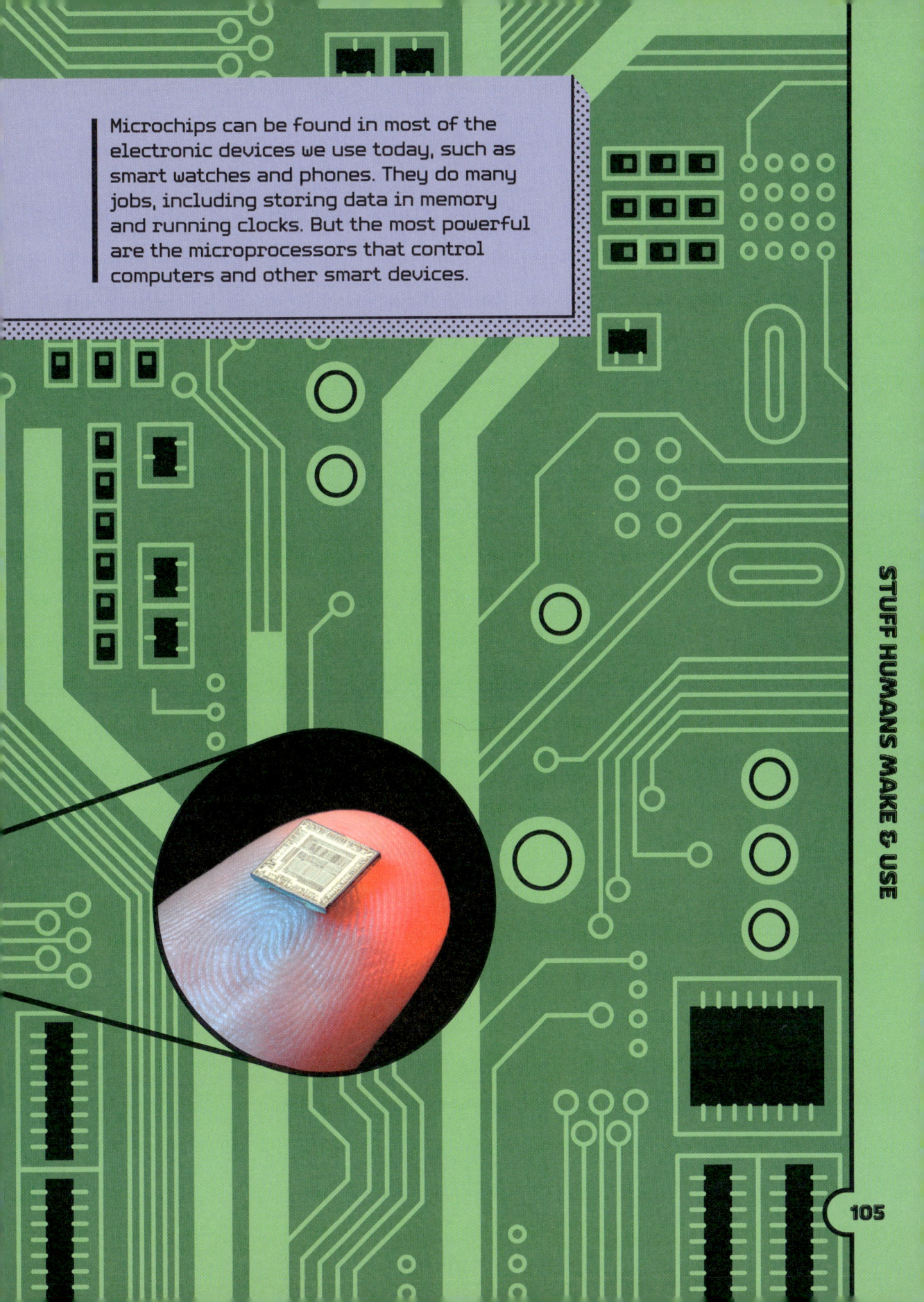

Microchips can be found in most of the electronic devices we use today, such as smart watches and phones. They do many jobs, including storing data in memory and running clocks. But the most powerful are the microprocessors that control computers and other smart devices.

STUFF HUMANS MAKE & USE

MICS & SPEAKERS

Sound is a fascinating thing, partly because it's a mix of matter and energy. It is caused by matter (such as your vocal cords or a musical instrument) vibrating, and it travels in pulses of motion energy called sound waves through solids, liquids and gases. When sound waves hit our eardrums, the energy causes them to vibrate, too, and nerves pass those signals to our brain. And for most of human history, that was that.

Beginning in the 1800s, inventors created telephones, radio, movies and more. These all used microphones and speakers to record and transmit sound. Then, starting in the mid-1900s, the world went digital, and now everything those earlier inventions allowed can be done with a single piece of technology – a smartphone – which, of course, can do lots of other, non-sound-related things, too. The crazy thing is this: even with all of that change, microphones and speakers work in pretty much the same way they did 150 years ago.

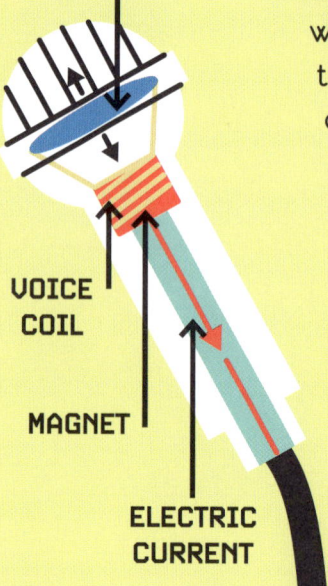

DIAPHRAGM
VOICE COIL
MAGNET
ELECTRIC CURRENT
AMPLIFIER

106

Microphone

In some microphones, sound waves (often music or speech) push against a thin membrane called a diaphragm. The diaphragm moves a coil of wire called a voice coil back and forth around a magnet. This creates pulses of electricity. If the microphone is attached to a computer or other storage device, the electric current goes through a converter that translates it into a digital series of 1s and 0s for storage. If not, it goes right to an amplifier which boosts the signal so that it can play through a speaker.

Speaker

Speakers are essentially the opposite of microphones. In a speaker, electrical impulses cause a voice coil inside a magnet to move back and forth. The coil is attached to a diaphragm that pushes against the air, producing sound waves that move out through the cone of the speaker towards your ear, where they vibrate your eardrum. If the sound was digitally recorded, the process starts with a converter changing the 1s and 0s to electric current.

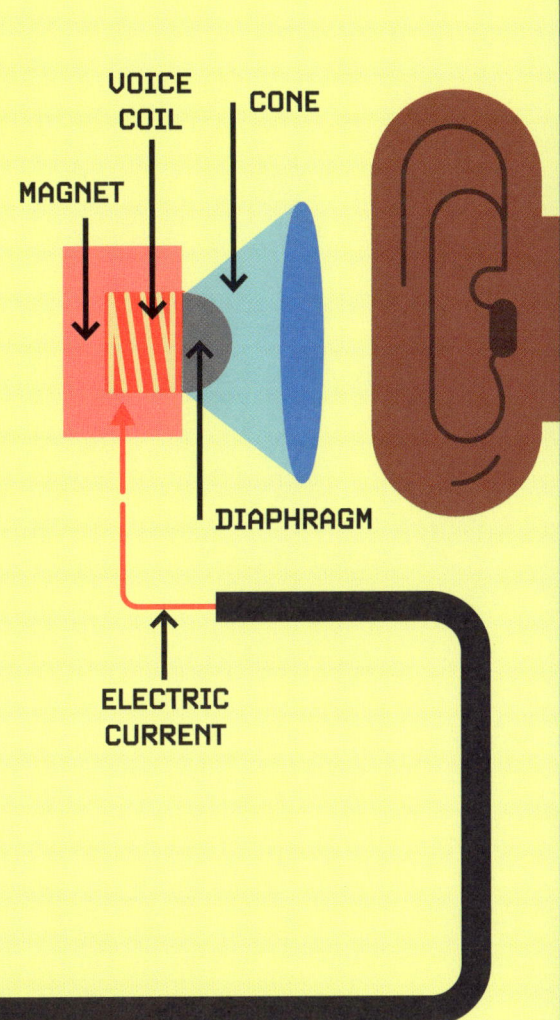

STUFF HUMANS MAKE & USE

107

CONNECTIONS

We humans are more connected than ever before, with our mobile devices letting us communicate with anyone at any time. But did you know that we owe all of this connectivity to radio waves, the electromagnetic radiation with the slowest vibrations (see page 37)? Humans have been using them since the very end of the 1800s, first for sending Morse code signals and then for transmitting voices, music and other sounds, plus visuals and data, over long distances. We also detect radio waves from space so we can learn about the universe.

And it is radio waves that transmit wireless phone calls. When you make a call, the microphone converts your voice into electrical impulses that are fed into a microchip that converts them to radio waves. These then leave the phone via a transmitter and travel to a cell tower, which then passes the signal on until it reaches the receiver in the phone of the person you are calling. There, the radio waves are converted back into electrical impulses that trigger the speaker in your friend's phone to make sound. And all at the speed of light.

Radio waves are also what allow you to send and receive data, from texts to streaming video, over mobile, satellite, wifi or Bluetooth systems.

BONUS!

Hedy Lamarr, a famous movie star from the 1900s, was also an inventor. She helped develop the technology that led to today's wifi.

Phone masts are sometimes disguised to make them fit into the landscape. This one is supposed to look like a pine tree.

STUFF HUMANS MAKE & USE

109

PROBLEMS WITH STUFF

Over the last 2 million years, we humans and our ancestors have made great strides in understanding the nature of matter and energy, which has allowed us to develop lots of amazing new stuff. But these positive developments have also led to some really bad stuff that's messing up our planet.

The news isn't all bad, though! Scientists and engineers are working on fixing many of the problems that we have caused, and part of the solution is coming up with new ways of making stuff! Here are a few areas where people are already making a difference in solving some of our biggest problems.

BONUS!

Currently humans on Earth generate more than 2 billion tonnes of municipal rubbish each year.

The Problem of Packaging

A big chunk of the rubbish we make comes from materials that package the things we buy. Containers made of paper, cardboard, metal, glass and plastic all need to be disposed of when they are empty. Plastic is especially dangerous because it breaks down into tiny microplastics that many animals and even people end up eating. →

Microplastics can end up in our bodies and cause us health problems in the future.

Many foods we buy don't need a big package, so now that we understand the risks, lots of people are choosing to buy food with less packaging.

How we can fix it!

The best way of getting rid of waste is to make less of it. Reducing packaging and using reusable bags to carry it home can eliminate lots of rubbish. Programs to recycle paper, glass, metal and plastics are becoming much more common. So are programs to compost food, as well as garden and agricultural wastes, turning them back into productive soil.

STUFF HUMANS MAKE & USE

111

Nuclear Waste

One of the most amazing discoveries that humans have made is how to tap into the energy released when atoms split apart. This process, called nuclear fission, can generate electricity without having to burn fossil fuels. (Go to page 19 for more on nuclear fission.) That's great for avoiding climate change, but there's a problem. Nuclear fission produces dangerous waste products which stay radioactive for thousands of years. Scientists have yet to come up with a way to safely dispose of nuclear waste, so it often just keeps piling up with no place to go. ⟶

Nuclear waste is often stored in barrels underground and far from people until we can figure out what to do with it.

Part of a closed nuclear powerplant in Germany in the midst of being destroyed.

How we can fix it!

New sources of energy such as wind and solar power are already making a dent in the amount of greenhouse gases we produce. As more clean energy becomes available, it is also allowing some countries to retire old nuclear power plants. Hydrogen and other options, such as nuclear fusion (see page 19) and using bacteria to make a fuel called methanol, could help, too.

Climate-Changing Food

We need to eat food to stay alive and healthy, but raising chickens, pigs, and cows requires a lot of energy and releases greenhouse gases into the air. As you know, these gases have been building up in our atmosphere, where they are changing the climate. We need to reduce our use of meat as our main food source as quickly as possible to help reverse global warming before it's too late. ➔

Cattle digest their tough food by fermenting it in their bellies. The result is lots of burps, each one adding to the methane in our atmosphere.

This burger is delicious, nutritious, and helps fight climate change. It's made with peas, chickpeas and corn, along with seasonings.

How we can fix it!

The simplest answer is to eat less meat and dairy and more fruits, vegetables, nuts, beans, and grains. For people who love meat, scientists are developing many new plant-based foods that taste like meat, providing us with a way to reduce our impact on Earth's climate and still have the tastes we like best. The bonus? A plant-based diet may actually be healthier for us anyway.

STUFF HUMANS MAKE & USE

Comets, dark matter, asteroids, meteorites, acids, crystals, gems, extremophiles, fossils, simple machines, boomerangs, musical instruments, paint, shoes, explosives, boats, fertilisers, maps, money, telescopes, hydrocarbons, petrochemicals, glass, adhesives, ceramics, mirrors, lenses, clocks, lightbulbs, thermometers, transistors, aeroplanes, blimps, photography, sonar, submarines, alloys, video displays, x-rays, rockets, scuba, nuclear reactors, lasers, radar, artificial intelligence, GMOs, nanotubes, satellites, superconductors...

BUT THERE'S MORE STUFF!

Well, here we are at the end of our journey, and we have covered lots of stuff. But I wish this were a longer book, because there is so much more I wanted to include. Also, I wish I could update it every year. Scientists and engineers are continuously coming up with new kinds of stuff to make our lives better, so there will be always be more stuff to discover.

Just to give you a taste of my struggle, here you can see a bunch of the things I wanted to put in but didn't have room for or could only mention briefly. You might want to find out about some of this stuff on your own.

Enjoy the adventure!

GLOSSARY

AIR PRESSURE The weight of Earth's atmosphere pressing down on it. Changing air pressure creates wind.

ALLOY A mixture of metals or a mixture of a metal with another element. Steel is an alloy that is made by combining iron and carbon.

AMPLIFIER A device that increases the electrical current flowing to a speaker, which allows the sound to be loud enough.

ATMOSPHERE The air surrounding Earth.

ATOM The smallest unit of a chemical element. Atoms are made of subatomic particles, which include protons, neutrons and electrons.

BIG BANG The moment at the beginning when the universe began and expanded from a spec too small to see to all of the stars, planets and galaxies there are.

BIOMEDICAL ENGINEERING Using technology to solve medical problems.

CELLS The building blocks of life. Some living things are just one cell while others are made up of trillions of them.

CHARCOAL Wood that has been burned slowly with very little oxygen. The 'coals' you see in your fireplace are actually charcoal. If you take away all of the oxygen from charcoal, it will stop burning and can be stored and used later as fuel.

CHEMISTRY A science that deals with atoms and the way they join together and split apart.

CHLOROPHYLL A green pigment in the cells of plants and some microorganisms that absorbs energy from sunlight to use in photosynthesis. It is also what makes plants green.

CIRCUIT (ELECTRICAL) A closed loop of conductors that includes a source of power and a device that needs powering.

COMBUSTION Fire.

CONDENSATION A gas, such as water vapour, turning into a liquid, such as water. Condensation takes place in clouds and also on the outside of a glass of ice water.

DENSITY A measurement that tells us how much matter is in a specific amount of space. If a lot of matter is packed into a space, it has high density. If less matter is in the same space, it has lower density.

DIESEL FUEL A heavy oil made from petroleum or organic matter and used to power motor vehicles and make electricity.

DIRT (SEE SOIL)

DNA (deoxyribonucleic acid) The molecule that acts like an instruction manual in the cells of living things, telling them how to develop and function.

EDIBLE Safe to eat.

ELECTRICAL Having to do with moving electrons.

ELECTRICAL CURRENT A stream of electrons flowing through a conductor.

ELECTROLYTE (BATTERY) A substance that allows charged ions to pass between a battery's cathode and the anode.

ELECTROMAGNETIC SPECTRUM The full range of electromagnetic waves, from very rapidly vibrating gamma waves to slower visible light to even slower radio waves.

ELECTRONS Negatively charged particles that orbit the nucleus in an atom. Electrons also exist outside of atoms. The movement of electrons is called 'electricity'.

ELEMENT (CHEMICAL) A substance made up of a single kind of atom.

ENERGY The stuff that makes matter move and change.

ENZYME A type of protein made by the body that starts or speeds up body processes. Amylase is an enzyme in your spit that helps break starches (like those in bread) into sugars.

FLAMMABLE Burns easily.

FOSSIL Remains or traces of an ancient living thing preserved, usually in stone.

FOSSIL FUEL A fuel created underground over millions of years through pressure and heat acting on the remains of living things. Oil, coal and natural gas are all fossil fuels.

FRESHWATER Water with a low salt content. Lakes, rivers, streams, and glaciers all contain freshwater.

FUEL Something that is burned to release its energy.

GRAVITY A force that pulls things together. The more massive an object, the more it pulls other objects towards it.

GREENHOUSE GAS A gas that traps heat in the atmosphere, keeping Earth warm.

HORMONE A substance made by the body that travels in body fluids (mostly blood) and makes things happen far from where they are made. Insulin, which moves sugar from our blood into our body's cells to make energy, is one of many hormones in our bodies.

ICE AGE One of several time periods during which much of Earth was covered by glaciers.

IGNITE Set on fire.

INSULATED Covered with a substance that keeps heat or cold in.

INSULATION A substance that blocks heat from moving from one side of it to the other.

ION An atom or a compound that has either gained or lost electrons. Ions are either negatively or positively charged.

LAVA Liquid rock when it comes out onto the surface of Earth.

LIGAMENT A band of tissue in the body of an animal that connects bones to one another but still allows the joints to bend.

MACRONUTRIENTS Stuff that you need to eat in large amounts to stay healthy.

MAGMA Liquid rock under the surface of Earth.

MAGNET A piece of metal where most of the electrons are spinning in the same direction. A magnet attracts iron and some other metals. A magnet suspended so it can move will line up with Earth's magnetic field and point north-south.

MASS A measure of how much stuff is found in something. On Earth, we calculate the mass of an object by weighing it on a scale.

MATTER Something made of atoms. Matter takes up space and has mass. The four common states of matter are solid, liquid, gas and plasma.

MICROBES (SEE MICROORGANISMS)

MICROBIOME An ecosystem made up of microorganisms. There are microbiomes everywhere on Earth, including inside our bodies.

MICROCHIP A tiny piece of silicon with electrical circuits etched into it. The microchip is the basis for modern computers.

MICRONUTRIENTS Stuff we need to eat in small amounts to stay healthy.

MICROORGANISMS ('MICROBES' FOR SHORT) Living things so small that humans can only see them by using a microscope.

MINERAL A substance that forms crystals. Quartz, calcite, feldspar, salt and ice are examples of minerals.

MOLECULE More than one atom that share electrons. When atoms join this way, they can become a whole different kind of stuff. For example, if two hydrogen atoms join with one oxygen atom, they become water.

mRNA (MESSENGER RIBONUCLEIC ACID) The molecule that copies individual instructions from DNA and carries them to where they can be followed.

NEBULA A giant cloud of dust and gas left over after a star has died, and also where new stars and solar systems are born.

NUCLEAR Having to do with the central structure of something. Nuclear power is power released from the nucleus of an atom.

NUCLEUS (CHEMISTRY) The centre of the atom, which is made up of positively charged protons and can contain neutral neutrons.

NUCLEUS (BIOLOGY) The control centre of the cell, where the DNA is stored.

NUTRIENTS The substances that living things need in their bodies to grow and thrive. Vitamins, minerals, fats, carbohydrates and proteins are all nutrients.

ORE Rock that contains valuable materials such as metals.

ORGANIC MATTER The material of living things, both alive and dead. Organic material is rich in carbon.

ORGANISM Living thing.

PETROL A mixture of fossil fuels processed into a liquid to power motor vehicles.

PHOTOSYNTHESIS The method by which plants use sunlight to transform water and the gas carbon dioxide into the sugar glucose. When plants do this, they give off oxygen, which we breathe.

PIGMENT A substance that gives something its colour.

PLANET A clump of matter orbiting a star that is large enough to form into a ball and has cleared its orbit of smaller clumps of matter.

POLAR (CHEMISTRY) Having a positively charged end and a negatively charged end.

POLAR (GEOGRAPHY) Refers to the areas around Earth's North and South Poles.

POLYMER A very long molecule made up of many repeating smaller units.

PROPERTY A category that describes how something looks or behaves. Mass, size, shape, taste and texture are all properties.

RADIANT Giving off energy, often in the form of light or heat.

RADIOACTIVE Describes a substance whose atoms are breaking down and giving off heat and radiation that is often dangerous to living things.

SEDIMENT Tiny bits of rock, dirt and organic matter that is blown, washed or pushed elsewhere.

SOIL A mix of sediment, organic matter, water and microorganisms. Most plants need soil to grow.

SOLAR SYSTEM A star and all of the objects (including planets, dwarf planets, asteroids, comets and moons) that are held together by its gravitational pull.

SPECTRUM A range of something. At one end of the human size spectrum are tiny babies, on the other end are basketball players and sumo wrestlers.

SPOKES (WHEEL) The bars that connect the hub (centre) of a wheel to its rim.

STAR A huge ball of glowing plasma that is constantly converting parts of itself into energy.

SUPERNOVA The explosion of a large dying star.

SYNTHETIC Artificial, not occurring in nature.

TENDON A rope-like tissue in an animal's body that attaches a muscle to something else (often a bone) and helps the muscle pull on that other thing.

THERMAL Having to do with heat.

TROPICAL Refers to the area of Earth on and near the equator.

UNIVERSE Everything that exists.

VIBRATION A rapid back-and-forth (or up-and-down) motion.

VOLCANIC VENT A place where lava and gases emerge from Earth.

WATER VAPOUR The gas form of water.

NOTE ON THE RESEARCH

Since this book covers so much stuff, researching it required a multi-faceted approach. To get the basic facts, I started with some very traditional sources, including encyclopaedias, science textbooks and journal articles. And of course I used websites.

Getting facts from the internet is always a bit tricky because you must verify that the website that you are using is legitimate and that the information is accurate. My procedure is to make sure any website I use is from a highly respected organisation that takes accuracy seriously. I then cross-reference the specific information I want to use with at least two other authoritative sources. When three reliable sources agree, I feel confident that I can share what I've learned with my readers.

In addition, for this book I spent a great deal of time visiting museums and speaking directly with experts (special thanks to Emily Bruno). Then, finally, once the writing was done, my editor hired an amazing fact-checker named Elizabeth Atalay go through the entire book and check every fact against several additional reliable sources just to make sure I hadn't picked up any errors by mistake.

There isn't room to list all of the sources Elizabeth and I used here, but I've included as many as I can over the next couple of pages.

SELECTED SOURCES

ACHRE Report, US Department of Energy Office of Environment, Health, Safety and Security (ehss.energy.gov/ohre/roadmap/achre/)

Advanced Earth and Space Sciences (agupubs.onlinelibrary.wiley.com)

Advanced Research Projects Agency-Energy (ARPA-E) (arpa-e.energy.gov)

Almanac (almanac.com)

American Chemical Society (ACS) (acs.org)

American Heart Association (heart.org)

American Museum of Natural History (amnh.org)

APS News, American Physical Society (aps.org/publications/apsnews/)

Archaeology (archaeology.org)

Archaeology Now (archaeologynow.org)

Astronomy Magazine (astronomy.com)

The Atlantic (theatlantic.com)

BBC (British Broadcasting Corporation) (bbc.co.uk)

Better Health Channel, Victoria, Australia (betterhealth.vic.gov.au/)

British Museum (britishmuseum.org)

British Society for Cell Biology (bscb.org/learning-resources/softcell-e-learning/chemistry-and-cells)

Brookhaven National Laboratory Newsroom (bnl.gov/newsroom/)

CAES Newswire, College of Agricultural & Environmental Sciences, University of Georgia (newswire.caes.uga.edu)

Car and Driver (caranddriver.com)

Carbon Brief (carbonbrief.org)

Centers for Disease Control and Prevention (CDC) (cdc.gov)

Ceramic Tech Today, American Ceramic Society (ceramics.org/feature/ceramic-tech-today/)

CERN (learn.cern/science)

Chemical & Engineering News (cen.acs.org)

Cleveland Clinic (my.clevelandclinic.org/health)

CU Today, University of Colorado Boulder (colorado.edu/today/)

Discover Magazine (discovermagazine.com)

Earth Magazine (earthmagazine.org)

Earth.org (earth.org)

EarthSky (earthsky.org)

Education and Outreach Collections from the University of Chicago (ecuip.lib.uchicago.edu)

Electronics Tutorials (electronics-tutorials.ws)

Encyclopaedia Britannica (britannica.com, kids.britannica.com)

Energy Education, University of Calgary (energyeducation.ca)

eSchool Today (eschooltoday.com)

Exploratorium (exploratorium.edu)

Exploring Our Fluid Earth, College of Education, University of Hawaii (manoa.hawaii.edu/exploringourfluidearth)

Forbes (forbes.com)

Frontline (frontline.thehindu.com/science-and-technology/)

Global Cold Chain Alliance (gcca.org/)

Great Lakes Worm Watch, University of Minnesota Duluth (wormwatch.d.umn.edu)

Green Cars (greencars.com)

Harvard Gazette (news.harvard.edu/gazette/)

Heart Matters, British Heart Foundation (bhf.org.uk/)

History (history.com)

How Stuff Works (howstuffworks.com)

Imperial College London (imperial.ac.uk/news/)

The Independent (independent.co.uk/news/science)

International Atomic Energy Agency (iaea.org)

121

Iowa State University Center for Nondestructive Evaluation (nde-ed.org)

JLab Science Education (education.jlab.org/)

Learn Genetics, University of Utah (learn.genetics.utah.edu/)

Lemelson-MIT Invention Education (lemelson.mit.edu/)

LibreTexts Chemistry, University of Kentucky (chem.libretexts.org/)

Live Science (livescience.com)

Maldwyn Montgomeryshire Wildlife Trust (montwt.co.uk)

Manhattan Institute (manhattan.institute)

Mayo Clinic (mayoclinic.org)

McGill University Office of Science and Society (mcgill.ca/oss/)

Medline Plus (medlineplus.gov)

Merriam-Webster Dictionary (merriam-webster.com)

Metropolitan Museum of Art (metmuseum.org)

Microbiome Journal (microbiomejournal.biomedcentral.com)

Minerals Education Coalition (mineralseducationcoalition.org)

MIT News, Massachusetts Institute of Technology (news.mit.edu)

Molecular Expressions, Florida State University (micro.magnet.fsu.edu)

The Morgan Library and Museum (themorgan.org)

NASA (astrobiology.nasa.gov, climate.nasa.gov, climatekids.nasa.gov, earthobservatory.nasa.gov, gpm.nasa.gov, hubblesite.org, imagine.gsfc.nasa.gov, nasa.gov, science.nasa.gov)

National Geographic (education.nationalgeographic.org)

National Human Genome Research Institute, NIH (genome.gov)

National Institute of Health (nih.gov)

National Museum of the American Indian, Smithsonian Institution (americanindian.si.edu)

National Nanotechnology Institute (nano.gov)

National Oceanic and Atmospheric Association (NOAA) (oceanservice.noaa.gov, mwrfc.noaa.gov, ncei.noaa.gov, climate.gov, weather.gov)

Native Seeds/SEARCH (nativeseeds.org)

Nature (nature.com)

NBC News (nbcnews.com)

New Scientist (newscientist.com)

New York Times (nytimes.com)

Our World in Data (ourworldindata.org)

Phinizy Center for Water Sciences (phinizycenter.org)

Phys.org (phys.org)

Physics Van, The Grainger College of Engineering, University of Illinois Urbana-Champaign (van.physics.illinois.edu)

PLOS Biology (journals.plos.org/plosbiology/)

PNAS (pnas.org)

Public Broadcasting Service (PBS) (pbs.org)

RMI (rmi.org)

Rock & Gem (rockngem.com)

Sapiens Anthropology Magazine (sapiens.org)

Science Direct (sciencedirect.com)

Science Learning Hub (sciencelearn.org.nz)

Science (science.org)

Science News Explores (snexplores.org)

Science Notes (sciencenotes.org)

Sciencing (sciencing.com)

Scientific American (scientificamerican.com)

Scitable by Nature Education (nature.com/scitable/)

Smithsonian American Art Museum (americanart.si.edu)

Smithsonian Magazine (smithsonianmag.com)

Smithsonian Science Education Center (ssec.si.edu)

Soil Science Society of America (soils4teachers.org)

Stanford Medicine Magazine (stanmed.stanford.edu)

Statista (statista.com)

Study.com (study.com)

ThoughtCo. (thoughtco.com)

Time (time.com)

UCAR Center for Science Education (scied.ucar.edu/)

UChicago News (news.uchicago.edu)

US Department of Energy, Office of Energy Efficiency & Renewable Energy (energy.gov/eere/), Office of Science (energy.gov/science/)

US Department of Agriculture, Natural Resources Conservation Service (nrcs.usda.gov)

US Energy Information Administration (eia.gov)

US Environmental Protection Agency (epa.gov/environmental-topics)

US Geological Survey (usgs.gov)

Washington Post (washingtonpost.com)

Wisconsin Plasma Experience, University of Wisconsin-Madison (plasmaexperience.engr.wisc.edu)

World Atlas (worldatlas.com)

World Heath Organization (who.int/news-room/)

World History Encyclopedia (worldhistory.org)

PHOTO CREDITS

The publisher would like to thank the following for permission to reproduce their photographs and illustrations. While every effort has been made to credit images, the publisher apologises for any errors or omissions and will be pleased to make any necessary corrections in future editions of the book.

Cover images: wheel Nastco/iStock.com, microphone Vermette/iStock.com, carrots harneshkp/iStock.com

p. 4 lechatnoir/iStock.com; **p. 17** tl WildMedia/Alamy, br Brozova/iStock.com; **p. 18** tl Greg Balfour Evans/Alamy, br by Zigmar Stein/AdobeStock.com; **p. 19** tl SeventyFour Images/Alamy, br Thiago Trevisan/Alamy; **p. 26** WitR/iStock.com; **p. 29** sciencephotos/Alamy; **p. 39** NASA/Alamy; **p. 51** Videologia/iStock.com; **p. 60** bl fcafotodigital/iStock.com, cr Marilyn Barbone/Shutterstock; **p. 61** bl alle12/iStock.com, tr carlosgaw/iStock.com; **p. 63** Nikada/iStock.com; **p. 65** MET/BOT/Alamy; **p. 66** bl Spaxia/Dreamstime.com, cr lapandr/123RF.com; **p. 67** bl kelllll/iStock.com, tr Eyewave/Dreamstime.com; **p. 69** ClassicStock/Alamy; **p. 72** bl Stock87/iStock.com, cr xijian/iStock.com; **p. 73** bl Mailson Pignata/iStock.com, tr Pacific Press Media Production Corp./Alamy; **p. 80** cl Bogdanhoda/iStock.com, br microstocker/iStock.com; **p. 81** tl kali9/iStock.com, br geogphotos/Alamy; **p. 82** Maticsandra/Dreamstime.com; **p. 84** cl Angelique Nijssen/iStock.com, br rvimages/iStock.com; **p. 85** tl GrigoriosMoraitis/iStock.com, br Nopparat Promtha/iStock.com; **p. 86** bl Museum and Galleries of Ljubljana, photo: Andrej Peunik, br Nastco/iStock.com; **p. 87** bl mariusFM77/iStock.com, br alexfan32/Shutterstock; **p. 88** duncan1890/iStock.com; **p. 89** tl LOC Photo/Alamy, br Bill Waterson/Alamy; **p. 92** ferrantraite/iStock.com; **p. 93** image by Patrice Audet from Pixabay; **p. 95** bg Viorika/iStock.com; **p. 101** Hispanolistic/iStock.com; **p. 102** ChooChin/iStock.com; **p. 103** bl AnnaStills/iStock.com, tr Dr Antonios Keirouz; **p. 105** inset Szasz-Fabian Jozsef/Shutterstock; **p. 109** Susan Vineyard /Alamy; **p. 111** bl pcess609/iStock.com, tr Marlon Trottmann/iStock.com; **p. 112** bl Enrico Salvadori/Alamy, tr dpa picture alliance/Alamy; **p. 113** bl Joel Masson/iStock.com, tr Marko Jan/iStock.com

INDEX

A
Aeroplanes 89
Air 4-5, 11, 18, 21, 35, 38-43, 50, 54, 66, 71, 72-73, 87, 96-97, 107, 113
Air pressure 38-39
Alcohol 73, 97
Alloy 81
Alternative energy 72-73
Analgesics 100
Anaesthesia 100-101
Aspirin 100
Atmosphere 40-43, 72, 112-113
Atoms 9, 10-15, 19, 22, 24, 28, 33, 42, 112

B
Bacteria 30, 35, 44, 46, 48, 54, 62, 66, 67, 97, 98, 112
Batteries 18, 76-77, 89, 103
Bi Sheng 92
Big Bang 22
Boats 86, 88
Boiling 65, 66, 88, 91, 94
Books 5, 90-93
Bricks 80
Bridges 81
Buildings 4, 26, 57, 73, 78-81

C
Canning 66
Carbohydrates 48, 60-61, 62
Carbon 13, 24, 42, 48, 70-71, 73, 81
Carbon dioxide 38, 40, 42, 50, 52, 71, 73
Cells 44, 47, 48-53, 55, 60, 61, 98-99, 103
Cement 80
Charge (negative and positive) 11, 12, 14, 33, 42, 77
Chemical bonds 14-15, 18, 33, 52
Chloroplasts 48-49, 50-51, 52
Circuit (electrical) 76-77, 104-105
Climate change 40-41, 71, 112-113
Clothing 4, 5, 57, 82-85, 94
Clouds 35, 42
Cold chain 68
Combustion (*see* Fire and Engines)

Continents 26, 88
Compass 28
Compounds (chemical) 14-15, 33
Computer 103, 104-105, 107
Concrete 80
Condensation 35
Cooking 17, 18, 21, 36, 57, 62-65, 70
Corn 30, 58, 73, 113
Cotton 82, 84
Covid-19 96, 99
Crystals 27, 46

D
Dehydration of food 67
Dirt 21, 27, 30-31, 35, 54-55, 64, 94-95, 111
Disinfectants 96-97, 98
DNA (deoxyribonucleic acid) 46-47, 48-49, 52-53, 99
Dunlop, John 87

E
Edison, Thomas 89
Ecosystems 34
Electric vehicles 89
Electrical generators 72, 74-75, 76
Electricity 11, 16, 17, 18, 19, 42, 70, 72, 74-77, 89, 104-105, 106-107, 108, 112
Electromagnetic radiation 36, 108
Electrons 12-15, 19, 22, 28, 42, 74, 76-77
Elements (chemical) 12-15, 22, 24, 26-27, 30, 42, 48, 73, 81
Energy 9, 16-19, 21, 22, 24, 36, 41, 42, 44, 48, 50, 52-53, 55, 60-61, 62, 70-77, 106, 110, 112-113
Engines 88-89
Enzymes 60
Ethanol (*see* Alcohol)

F
Fabric 82-85
Faraday, Michael 74
Farming 58-59, 82

124

Fats (see Lipids)
Fire 17, 18, 42-43, 62-65, 88-89
Flax 84
Food 17, 18, 36, 38, 50, 55, 57, 58-69, 96, 111, 113
Franklin, Rosalind 46
Freshwater 32
Fuel 18, 19, 42, 70-73, 74, 88-89, 112
Fungi 30, 54, 67

G
Germs 55, 96-99
Global warming (see Climate change)
Glucose 48, 50, 52, 61
Gravity 18, 22, 24, 44, 72
Greenhouse effect 17, 40-41, 112-113
Gutenberg, Johannes 93

H
Health 54, 57, 58, 61-61, 94-103, 111, 113
Heat 16-19, 24, 35, 36, 40-41, 42, 62-65, 66, 68, 70, 73, 80, 92
Helium 13, 14, 22
Hormones 60
Human body 4, 24, 33, 38, 44, 45, 46, 48, 54-55, 60-61, 62, 78, 94-103, 113
Hurricanes 39
Hydrogen 14, 15, 22, 33, 42, 48, 73, 112

I
Ice 27, 32, 34, 54, 68-69
Ice ages 41
Ice box 68-69
Immune system 98-99
Ions 14
Iron 24, 26, 28-29, 48, 61, 76, 81, 87, 92

JK
Joint replacements 102
Kwolek, Stephanie 102

L
Lamarr, Hedy 108
Lava 26
Life and living things 17, 21, 32, 36, 38, 44-55, 70,
Light 4, 17, 18, 19, 22, 36-37, 40-41, 50, 52, 72
Lightning 11, 42-43

Linen 84, 91
Lipids 48, 60
Lister, Joseph 96
Lodestones (see Magnets)

M
Magma 26
Magnets 28-29, 74-75, 106-107
Mass 9, 10, 38, 48
Matter 9, 10-15, 16, 18, 21, 24-25, 38, 42, 44, 50, 106, 110
Metal 14, 27, 28-29, 76, 81, 86, 93, 111,
Methane 40, 113
Microbes 50, 52, 54-55, 58, 66, 68, 96-97 (see also Bacteria)
Microbiome 54
Microchips 104-105, 108
Microphones 106-107
Microplastics 111
Microscope 54, 96
Minerals 27, 30, 60-61, 80
Mitochondria 48-49, 52-53
Molecules 9, 15, 33, 42, 46-47, 61, 73, 81, 94-95, 99
Moore, Ruth Ella 97
Motors 19, 88-89
Mould 66, 67, 98
mRNA (messenger ribonucleic acid) 48, 99

N
Nebula 24-25
Nuclear energy (fission and fusion) 16, 19, 24, 112
Nuclear waste 112
Nucleus (of an atom) 12-13, 19, 28, 42
Nucleus (of a cell) 47-49, 52
Nutrients 30-31, 55, 60-61, 62, 113
105, 210

O
Oceans 26, 32, 38-39, 54, 55
Organic matter 55, 70
Organisms (see Life and living things)
Ovens 64, 80
Oxygen 15, 24, 26, 33, 38, 42, 48, 50, 52-53, 66

PQ
Packaging 111
Painkillers 100-101
Paper 5, 90-93, 111
Papyrus 90
Petrol 88-89
Photosynthesis 17, 36, 38, 48, 50-51, 73
Pickling 66
Plants 17, 30, 36, 38, 48-49, 50-51, 55, 58-59, 70-71, 73, 82, 84
Plasma (state of matter) 10-11, 42
Plastic 81, 111
Polar molecule 33
Polymers 81, 103
Pottery 65
Printing 91, 92-93, 103
Prosthetics 103
Protein 47, 48, 60, 99
Pyramids 26

R
Radio waves 36-37, 108
Railways 88
Refrigeration 68-69
Rocks 2, 21, 26-29, 30, 44, 64, 65, 70, 79, 80
Rubber 87
Rubbish 110-111

S
Salt 14, 27, 66
Sediment 27, 30, 70
Sewing 82
Silicon 26, 104
Silk 85, 91
Smartphone 5, 104-105, 106
Smoking food 67
Soap 94-95, 97
Solar power 72, 73, 112
Solar system 4, 24-25, 26
Soil (see Dirt)
Sound 18, 104, 106-107, 108
Speakers 106-107, 108
Spinning yarn or thread 82-83, 85
Stars 10, 19, 21, 22, 24-25, 44
Static electricity 42, 74
Steam power 74, 88-89
Steel 17, 28, 81
Stephenson, George 88

Subatomic particles 12-13, 19, 22
Sun 10, 17, 19, 21, 22, 25, 35, 36-37, 42, 67, 80, 91 (see also Light)
Supernova 24

T
Trains (see Railways)
Trevithick, Richard 88
Ts'ai Lun 91
Type 92-93
Tyre 86-87

U
Universe 4, 22, 108

U
Vaccines 68, 98-99
Viruses 48, 54, 96-99
Vitamins 60-61
Volta, Alessandro 76-77

WXYZ
Water 5, 11, 15, 21, 27, 32-35, 42, 48, 50, 52, 54, 63, 65, 66-67, 72, 73, 86, 88, 91, 94-95, 97
Water cycle 35
Water vapour 35, 40
Weather 34, 35, 38-39, 40, 66, 78
Weathering 30
Wheels 86-87, 89
Wind 18, 27, 38-39, 72, 73, 86, 88, 112
Wireless communication 108-109
Wright Brothers 89
Wood 18, 42, 65, 70, 87, 91, 92
Wool 82, 85
X-rays 36

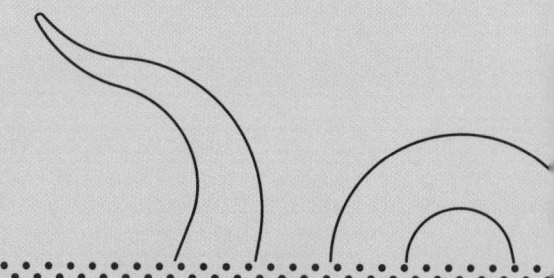

Fats (see Lipids)
Fire 17, 18, 42-43, 62-65, 88-89
Flax 84
Food 17, 18, 36, 38, 50, 55, 57, 58-69, 96, 111, 113
Franklin, Rosalind 46
Freshwater 32
Fuel 18, 19, 42, 70-73, 74, 88-89, 112
Fungi 30, 54, 67

G

Germs 55, 96-99
Global warming (see Climate change)
Glucose 48, 50, 52, 61
Gravity 18, 22, 24, 44, 72
Greenhouse effect 17, 40-41, 112-113
Gutenberg, Johannes 93

H

Health 54, 57, 58, 61-61, 94-103, 111, 113
Heat 16-19, 24, 35, 36, 40-41, 42, 62-65, 66, 68, 70, 73, 80, 92
Helium 13, 14, 22
Hormones 60
Human body 4, 24, 33, 38, 44, 45, 46, 48, 54-55, 60-61, 62, 78, 94-103, 113
Hurricanes 39
Hydrogen 14, 15, 22, 33, 42, 48, 73, 112

I

Ice 27, 32, 34, 54, 68-69
Ice ages 41
Ice box 68-69
Immune system 98-99
Ions 14
Iron 24, 26, 28-29, 48, 61, 76, 81, 87, 92

JK

Joint replacements 102
Kwolek, Stephanie 102

L

Lamarr, Hedy 108
Lava 26
Life and living things 17, 21, 32, 36, 38, 44-55, 70,
Light 4, 17, 18, 19, 22, 36-37, 40-41, 50, 52, 72
Lightning 11, 42-43

Linen 84, 91
Lipids 48, 60
Lister, Joseph 96
Lodestones (see Magnets)

M

Magma 26
Magnets 28-29, 74-75, 106-107
Mass 9, 10, 38, 48
Matter 9, 10-15, 16, 18, 21, 24-25, 38, 42, 44, 50, 106, 110
Metal 14, 27, 28-29, 76, 81, 86, 93, 111,
Methane 40, 113
Microbes 50, 52, 54-55, 58, 66, 68, 96-97 (see also Bacteria)
Microbiome 54
Microchips 104-105, 108
Microphones 106-107
Microplastics 111
Microscope 54, 96
Minerals 27, 30, 60-61, 80
Mitochondria 48-49, 52-53
Molecules 9, 15, 33, 42, 46-47, 61, 73, 81, 94-95, 99
Moore, Ruth Ella 97
Motors 19, 88-89
Mould 66, 67, 98
mRNA (messenger ribonucleic acid) 48, 99

N

Nebula 24-25
Nuclear energy (fission and fusion) 16, 19, 24, 112
Nuclear waste 112
Nucleus (of an atom) 12-13, 19, 28, 42
Nucleus (of a cell) 47-49, 52
Nutrients 30-31, 55, 60-61, 62, 113 105, 210

O

Oceans 26, 32, 38-39, 54, 55
Organic matter 55, 70
Organisms (see Life and living things)
Ovens 64, 80
Oxygen 15, 24, 26, 33, 38, 42, 48, 50, 52-53, 66

125

PQ

Packaging 111
Painkillers 100-101
Paper 5, 90-93, 111
Papyrus 90
Petrol 88-89
Photosynthesis 17, 36, 38, 48, 50-51, 73
Pickling 66
Plants 17, 30, 36, 38, 48-49, 50-51, 55, 58-59, 70-71, 73, 82, 84
Plasma (state of matter) 10-11, 42
Plastic 81, 111
Polar molecule 33
Polymers 81, 103
Pottery 65
Printing 91, 92-93, 103
Prosthetics 103
Protein 47, 48, 60, 99
Pyramids 26

R

Radio waves 36-37, 108
Railways 88
Refrigeration 68-69
Rocks 2, 21, 26-29, 30, 44, 64, 65, 70, 79, 80
Rubber 87
Rubbish 110-111

S

Salt 14, 27, 66
Sediment 27, 30, 70
Sewing 82
Silicon 26, 104
Silk 85, 91
Smartphone 5, 104-105, 106
Smoking food 67
Soap 94-95, 97
Solar power 72, 73, 112
Solar system 4, 24-25, 26
Soil (see Dirt)
Sound 18, 104, 106-107, 108
Speakers 106-107, 108
Spinning yarn or thread 82-83, 85
Stars 10, 19, 21, 22, 24-25, 44
Static electricity 42, 74
Steam power 74, 88-89
Steel 17, 28, 81
Stephenson, George 88
Subatomic particles 12-13, 19, 22
Sun 10, 17, 19, 21, 22, 25, 35, 36-37, 42, 67, 80, 91 (see also Light)
Supernova 24

T

Trains (see Railways)
Trevithick, Richard 88
Ts'ai Lun 91
Type 92-93
Tyre 86-87

U

Universe 4, 22, 108

V

Vaccines 68, 98-99
Viruses 48, 54, 96-99
Vitamins 60-61
Volta, Alessandro 76-77

WXYZ

Water 5, 11, 15, 21, 27, 32-35, 42, 48, 50, 52, 54, 63, 65, 66-67, 72, 73, 86, 88, 91, 94-95, 97
Water cycle 35
Water vapour 35, 40
Weather 34, 35, 38-39, 40, 66, 78
Weathering 30
Wheels 86-87, 89
Wind 18, 27, 38-39, 72, 73, 86, 88, 112
Wireless communication 108-109
Wright Brothers 89
Wood 18, 42, 65, 70, 87, 91, 92
Wool 82, 85
X-rays 36

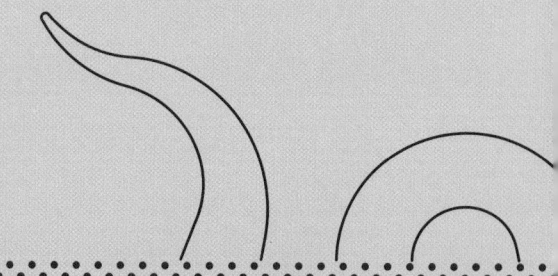

Life Key

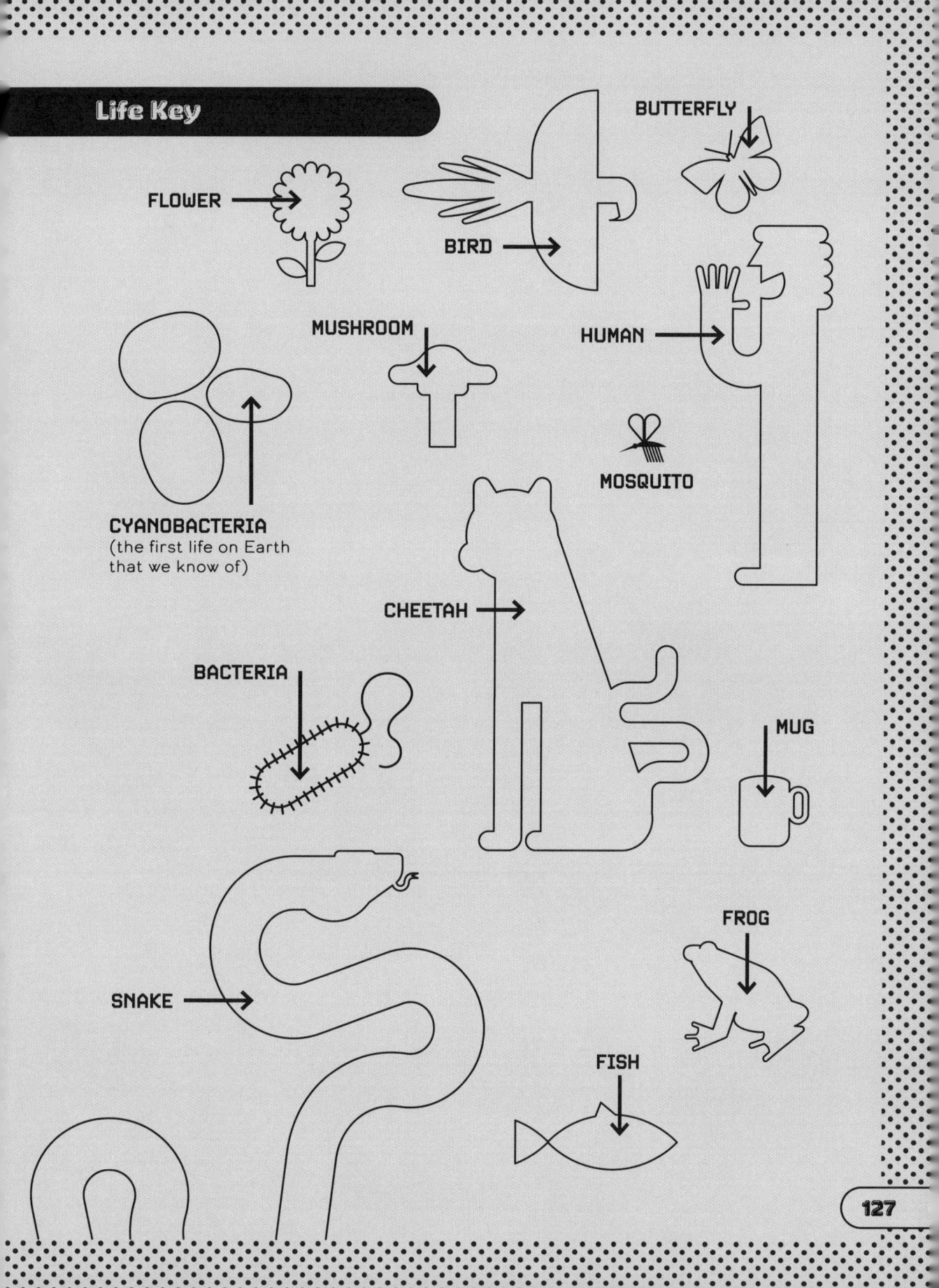

FLOWER

BUTTERFLY

BIRD

MUSHROOM

HUMAN

CYANOBACTERIA
(the first life on Earth that we know of)

MOSQUITO

CHEETAH

BACTERIA

MUG

SNAKE

FROG

FISH

What on Earth!

What on Earth! is an imprint of What on Earth Publishing
The Black Barn, Wickhurst Farm, Leigh, Tonbridge, Kent, UK, TN11 8PS
30 Ridge Road Unit B, Greenbelt, Maryland, 20770, United States

First published in the United Kingdom in 2025
Text copyright © 2025 Stephen M. Tomecek
Illustrations copyright © 2025 John Devolle

All rights reserved. No part of this publication may be reproduced or transmitted in any form or by any means, electronic or mechanical, including photocopying, recording, or any information storage or retrieval system, without permission in writing from the publishers. Requests for permission to make copies of any part of this work should be directed to contactus@whatonearthbooks.com.

Written by Steve Tomecek
Illustrated by John Devolle
Designed by Nell Wood

Staff for this book: Natalie Bellos, Publisher; Patrick Skipworth, Laura Buller and Nancy Feresten, Editors; Andy Forshaw, Art Director; Nell Wood, Senior Designer; Elizabeth Atalay, Fact-checker; Angela Modany, Charka Stout and Sophie Macintyre, Proofreaders; Lauren Fulbright, Production Manager

A CIP catalogue record for this book is available from the British Library

ISBN: 978-1-804661-41-3

LPP/Heshan, China/09/2024
Printed in China

1 3 5 7 9 10 8 6 4 2

whatonearthbooks.com

MIX
Paper | Supporting responsible forestry
FSC® C020056